teach®
yourself

how to write your
life story

how to write your life story

ann gawthorpe

Launched in 1938, the **teach yourself** series grew rapidly in response to the world's wartime needs. Loved and trusted by over 50 million readers, the series has continued to respond to society's changing interests and passions and now, 70 years on, includes over 500 titles, from Arabic and Beekeeping to Yoga and Zulu. What would you like to learn?

be where you want to be with **teach yourself**

For UK order enquiries: please contact Bookpoint Ltd, 130 Milton Park, Abingdon, Oxon OX14 4SB. Telephone: +44 (0) 1235 827720. Fax: +44 (0) 1235 400454. Lines are open 09.00–17.00, Monday to Saturday, with a 24-hour message answering service. Details about our titles and how to order are available at www.teachyourself.co.uk

For USA order enquiries: please contact McGraw-Hill Customer Services, PO Box 545, Blacklick, OH 43004-0545, USA. Telephone: 1-800-722-4726. Fax: 1-614-755-5645.

For Canada order enquiries: please contact McGraw-Hill Ryerson Ltd, 300 Water St, Whitby, Ontario L1N 9B6, Canada. Telephone: 905 430 5000. Fax: 905 430 5020.

Long renowned as the authoritative source for self-guided learning – with more than 50 million copies sold worldwide – the **teach yourself** series includes over 500 titles in the fields of languages, crafts, hobbies, business, computing and education.

British Library Cataloguing in Publication Data: a catalogue record for this title is available from the British Library.

Library of Congress Catalog Card Number: on file.

First published in UK 2009 by Hodder Education, part of Hachette UK, 338 Euston Road, London, NW1 3BH.

First published in US 2009 by The McGraw-Hill Companies, Inc.

This edition published 2009.

The **teach yourself** name is a registered trade mark of Hodder Headline.

Typeset by Transet Limited, (Printed in Great Britain for Road, London NW1 3BH, by

The publisher has used its be referred to in this book are c publisher and the author h guarantee that a site will rer appropriate.

Hachette UK's policy is to us and made from wood grow processes are expected to conform to the environmental regulations of the country of origin.

Impression number   10 9 8 7 6 5 4 3 2 1
Year   2012 2011 2010 2009

contents

dedication

This book is dedicated to my daughters, Nicola and Linda, and my granddaughters, Jasmine, Charlie, Anna and Alexandra, in the hope that they will all write their life stories some day.

acknowledgements

I would like to thank the following:

Lesley Bown for her support.

Anne Brooke, Sally Crocker, Mary Frances, Ian Henderson, Lori Lober, Mary Lucas, Edna Lydiate and Geoff Walford for allowing me to use their experiences as the case studies.

Elizabeth Ashworth, Christine Franklin, Scott Mariani, Valerie McConnell, Jane Rowland, Tony Staveacre, Helen Tovey and Lee Weatherly for providing words of wisdom at the beginning of the chapters.

I would also like to thank those who allowed me to use extracts from the following books:

Arthur's Village by Arthur Westcott, courtesy of Patricia Fox.

Burma Railway, Images of War by Jack Chalker, courtesy of Jack Chalker.

Lunch Meat and Life Lessons by Mary Lucas, courtesy of Mary Lucas.

Mike's Memoirs by 'Mike' Hunt, courtesy of Richard Hunt.

Song of the Spinning Sun by Mary Frances, courtesy of Mary Frances.

Unsettled by Graham Walker, courtesy of Graham Walker and Tangent Books.

Extracts from *I didn't get where I am Today* by David Nobbs, published by William Heinemann Ltd are reprinted by permission of The Random House Group Ltd. Extracts from *I didn't get where I am Today*, Copyright © David Nobbs 2003 are reprinted by kind permission of Jonathan Clowes Ltd., London, on behalf of David Nobbs.

Extracts from *Kilvert's Diary* by Francis Kilvert, published by Jonathan Cape are reprinted by kind permission of The Random House Group Ltd.

Extracts from *I'm a Teacher Get Me Out of Here* by Francis Gilbert, are reprinted by kind permission of Short Books.

The article *A Mod and her Scooter* is reprinted by kind permission of *Yours* magazine.

introduction

It is said that everybody has at least one book in them – and for most people that book will probably be their life story.

And if you are thinking, 'my life isn't interesting enough to write about', think again. Everyone's life is unique, only you have lived through that particular set of circumstances and felt those emotions. Your life is an important part of history and even if your story isn't written for general publication it will be interesting and valuable not only to your family and friends but also to future social historians – because you will be adding your own particular view of the events you have lived through and people you have known.

But, you may argue, 'I don't know how to write my life story' – don't worry, you probably already have. Each postcard you've sent detailing your holiday activities, each Christmas round robin bringing friends and family up to date with the year's events is a mini memoir.

While most of us probably won't write a blockbuster or that seminal novel of the twenty-first century, writing readable and interesting prose can be learned – so don't be put off from putting pen to paper or turning on the word processor. And if you are worried that your English isn't good enough or you are bad at grammar and can't tell a split infinitive from a split sausage – don't be. Grammar is not as rigid as it once was and this is your life story and should reflect how you speak. It is far better to be authentic than grammatical. But just in case, Chapter 14 includes some simple rules of grammar and how to avoid some common errors.

So what are life stories and how do they differ from autobiographies and memoirs? It is generally accepted that memoirs relate to a particular portion of your life whereas autobiographies and life stories start with your birth and go right up to the present time. Biographies cover the same ground but are written by someone else.

Having said that, the terms are somewhat interchangeable – life stories on blogging websites and in specialist magazines may cover one particular period of a person's life, and some books, which are called memoirs, may cover the whole of a person's life. I've mainly used the term life story throughout the book to cover all eventualities.

There are many reasons why people decide to write their life story. Some may have found some old diaries or letters which they think should be written down for the family. Others may want to tell their grandchildren what life was like when they were young, or to put the record straight for the public. Writing them may also be cathartic, particularly when it comes to the so called 'misery memoirs', which generally chart periods of appalling abuse.

As well as knowing why you want to write it is also important to know who you are writing for because this could affect the content. If you are writing for family and friends they will be interested in all the nitty-gritty details of family life, both past and present. If you are writing for the public then you will need to be more selective and only include the really interesting parts.

So, how do you set about writing one? Firstly, there is no right or wrong way to write a life story – you can write it in any way you want to. You can start at the beginning, in the middle or at the end. The important thing is to get started, to keep going and to finish it.

Unless you have total recall and have kept lengthy diaries most of us need a little help with remembering. Section one of this book includes tips on how to trigger memories and how to research background information which will add colour and texture to your story. There is also a chapter on how to research your family tree.

Section two is all about writing. Once you have collected all your information it is time to put pen to paper and there are many ways of writing a life story from the simple diary format to basing it on themes or topics.

There is also your style to consider; will your life story be formal, chatty or humorous. Most books benefit from a touch of humour, particularly if you are aiming at the wider public.

There is also a chapter on hints for making your life story a page-turner.

Once you have decided on the type of life story, who you are aiming it at and the style it will be written in, do you have the time and the willpower to actually write it? Writing a full-length book can be a daunting process, but so can knitting a jumper, making a wedding dress or building a house. The secret is to break these tasks down into manageable chunks. There are chapters on how to write up an anecdote for a magazine and how to overcome writer's block.

Unless you have been given a deadline by a publisher it is up to you how long you take and when and how often you write. Having said that, it is preferable to give yourself some kind of deadline to ensure your life story gets finished, so there are tips on finding time to write and how to use that time productively.

Some novels could be described as life stories written in the third person, so section three concentrates on how to fictionalize your life story and write it like a novel.

Section four is all about publishing. To be fair, few life stories are going to be picked up by traditional publishers, but that doesn't mean you can't produce a good quality book – it can even be done on a home computer.

Finally, section five shows how you can build on your achievements, from giving talks to becoming a biographer.

So far we have only talked about life stories written by one person, however there is nothing to stop them being jointly authored. Usually this is husband and wife, or partners. The advantages of this arrangement is there are two people to come up with the memories, share the research and help make the decisions on what to include and what to leave out. And if one author has to drop out the other one will be able to finish it. And there is no reason why the whole family shouldn't put pen to paper and combine their memories – it could make for some interesting reading if different viewpoints about a particular situation are all included.

Much of this book is based on my experiences helping my mother research, write and publish her memoirs at the age of 91. However, don't think that you have to be elderly to write your memoirs – anyone of any age will have something interesting to say about their life or at the very least a special part of it.

In fact, with the advent of blogging on the Internet – which is just writing your memoirs in real time – more and more young people are putting their life stories out there in the public domain. If you haven't yet tried blogging, section four shows you how to get started – but be warned some people find it addictive.

No book can write your life story for you – that is down to you. What I hope to do is to encourage you to have a go, give you some hints on how to go about it, and come up with some ideas you may not have thought of.

Writing your life story can be an exciting adventure. Memories will come flooding back, you will probably learn a lot more about your family roots and you may even get back in touch with friends and family who have been lost to you for years. It could also open up lots of other possibilities and may even lead to a new career in writing.

By looking at this book you have taken the first step – now take the second and start writing.

Good luck.

Ann

section one

collecting material

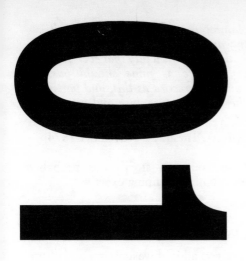

01

defining your reasons

In this chapter you will learn:
- why people write their life stories
- the different types of life story
- who they are written for.

Why do I keep this voluminous journal? I can hardly tell. Partly because life appears to me such a curious and wonderful thing that it almost seems a pity that even such a humble and uneventful life as mine should pass altogether away without some record as this, and partly too because I think the record may amuse and interest some who come after me.

The Rev Francis Kilvert, Tuesday 3 November 1874

Before you get started on your life story it is probably worthwhile spending a few moments defining exactly:

- why you want to write it
- what kind you want to write
- who you are writing it for.

In the long run this will save you a lot of wasted time and effort and will also help to ensure that your book has a coherent structure and framework. It's a bit like gardening – no one grabs a few packets of flower seeds, throws them out into the garden and hopes for the best. You decide what you want to grow and where you want to grow it. Then you prepare the soil for optimum results and thin out the plants so that those which are left make a great show.

Why you want to write it

Writing a life story can be a time-consuming business so before going any further it makes sense to clarify why you want to do it. Once you know why there is every chance you will finish it. If you can't decide why then there is a good chance you won't see it through to the end.

There are many reasons why people want to write their life story, including:

- always wanted to write a book
- invited to
- cathartic
- therapeutic
- benefits of your experience
- as a tribute
- urgent story to tell
- payment
- putting the record straight

- tit for tat
- fame
- kiss and tell.

Always wanted to write a book

Pick up any book about how to write a novel, play or a magazine article and one of the main pieces of advice is always to start by writing about what you know. And if there is one thing you do know a lot about it's your life – so where better to start your writing career than with writing your life story.

Don't forget, these don't have to be written as a chronological memoir or diary – like many other writers, you can fictionalize them to form the basis of a novel. (For more on how to do this see Chapters 14 and 15.)

Invited to

Many people start writing their life stories because family and friends have asked them to write down their experiences. Perhaps you have been asked by a local history group to share your memories. Or if you have worked for the same company for many years, or been a long time member of a sports club, orchestra or drama group you may have been invited to contribute your memories to their archives. Having written about this part of your life then perhaps you could extend it to include the rest.

Example:

Since the end of the war we have held annual 615 Squadron reunions at our home airfield, Kenley, and it was at one of these gatherings that I met up again with an old friend from the Squadron, Vic Milner, who was editor of our Squadron magazine. Vic told me how difficult it was to find material for the magazine. Knowing I had been a regular airman for many years and that I had served on Flying Boats, he suggested I should write something.

Vic told me that he liked what I sent him, and moreover that some of the magazine readers had liked it too, so would I please send him further episodes. From then on, like Topsy, it has kept on growing.

From *Mike's Memoirs* by Frank 'Mike' Hunt

Cathartic

Writing about our traumatic experiences can be a form of therapy. And don't forget, not only could you benefit from writing down your experiences, but they could also help others who may find themselves in a similar situation and think that they were the only ones going through it. If your story has an uplifting ending this will also give hope to others that there is a light at the end of the tunnel.

Example:

Jenny Tomlin's *Behind Closed Doors* is a harrowing story of child abuse and cruelty, but Jenny, who is the mother of UK actress Martine McCutcheon, not only survived with her spirit intact but is now a children's rights campaigner.

US writer, Dave Pelzer, who wrote *A Child called It*, which chronicles the years of abuse he suffered at the hands of his alcoholic mother before being rescued by his teachers, has gone on to write five more best-sellers, including *Help Yourself*, a book designed to encourage people to overcome past traumas and lead full and productive lives.

However, re-living terrible memories can also be traumatic so if you are contemplating writing a book about difficult experiences you may also want to consider seeking counselling.

The British Association for Counselling and Psychotherapy (BACP) will be able to provide you with a list of counsellors in your area who are members of the BACP and who will abide by its ethical rules of behaviour and respect your privacy.

You can contact them via their website **www.bacp.co.uk/** or ring 01455 883300 or email **bacp@bacp.co.uk** or write to: British Association for Counselling and Psychotherapy, BACP House, 15 St John's Business Park, Lutterworth, Leicestershire LE17 4HB.

To find a qualified counsellor in the USA contact the National Board for Certified Counselors (NBCC) on their website **www.nbcc.org** or ring 336 547 0607 or email **nbcc@nbcc.org** or write to: 33 Terrace Way, Greensboro, North Carolina, 27403 3360 USA.

Therapeutic

If you have suffered a traumatic experience such as nursing a loved one through a long illness, writing down your experiences could not only be a healing experience for you and help you to come to terms with what happened, but could also help others in a similar situation.

Benefits of your experience

If you have learned life's lessons the hard way then passing advice on to others may save them from making the same mistakes. If you have fought self-inflicted wounds like alcohol or drug abuse, telling others about your experiences and how you overcame them could help those who find themselves in a similar situation. These are always going to be 'warts and all' life stories, but if you can show that it is possible to come through the dark times and turn your life around this could give hope to your readers.

Or perhaps you have suffered from a chronic illness or debilitating condition in which case your experiences could be invaluable to others coping with the same problem.

Lori Lober, who with her husband runs a building company in Kansas City, had a compelling reason to write her life story.

Case study

I was diagnosed at stage four breast cancer a little over eight years ago. Although I was diagnosed at one of the leading cancer institutions in the world my dire prognosis gave me little or no hope. The exception was a spot available in a clinical trial that did offer me more hope than what was available via approved FDA treatment. I signed up for the clinical trial immediately and began my journey to wellness.

I understand how intense and wonderful Western medicine is but I also believe Eastern medicine warrants great consideration when you're facing a death sentence. I embraced the best of both types of medicine and created a 'journey to wellness' that has worked well for me. As other people were newly diagnosed with cancer they began asking what I was doing. At 18 months following my diagnosis instead of being dead I was alive and well and newly diagnosed as 'no evidence of disease'.

I want to be there for them at their time of need – that's what I wish I had at the time of my diagnosis. Someone who had been faced with the most severe stage of cancer but was alive and doing well. I began writing everything about my journey and then transformed those notes into *Bigger Than Pink*. Now that my journey is in writing, others who hear the dreaded words 'you have cancer' can read my story and decide for themselves what they would like to incorporate into their personal cancer journey. My goal was to reach out to others and if *Bigger Than Pink* helped only one person survive cancer my efforts were well worth it! Throughout the course of the last two years since my book has been published I have heard stories weekly about how others have embraced my words and it has truly changed their outlook and their cancer journey as a whole. Having others tell me how powerful *Bigger Than Pink* has been for them in their journey is the best feeling in the world and I wouldn't trade a day of my cancer journey and what I continue to learn from it.

Lori Lober

As a tribute

If you have met people whose bravery, courage or ideals have had a profound effect on your life then you may want to tell others about them and in doing so find you are writing about yourself as well.

Example:

Although Jack Chalker, author of *Burma Railway, Images of War,* had been pressed to write an account of his years as a Japanese Prisoner of War to support a large selection of his war drawings, it was written also, and dedicated, as a tribute to a great Australian surgeon and to others who had contributed so much to survival in the Thailand Railway Camps.

In Mitch Albom's *Tuesday's with Morrie: An Old Man, A Young Man and Life's Greatest Lesson* he writes about his weekly meetings with his former tutor from Brandeis University, Morrie Schwartz, who despite a degenerative illness which results in his death, shares with Mitch his thoughts on how to truly live.

Urgent story to tell

If something amazing has happened to you then you will want to share it with other people. This could be a religious experience, a fantastic adventure or perhaps finding love and romance in later life.

Example:

Mary Frances experienced an extraordinary religious moment which changed her life for ever, or as she puts it in her life story *Song of the Spinning Sun*, 'To be precise I went from unbelief in God to total belief in about 30 seconds.' Her book is about her journey from that moment on.

Payment

Don't be embarrassed by wanting to make money out of your life story. Dr Johnson said, 'No man but a blockhead ever wrote, except for money.' However, if your intention is to write for financial gain then you will need to make sure that your life story is saleable.

Putting the record straight

Many people feel they have been misunderstood or deliberately maligned at certain periods of their lives. Writing about those periods enables them to put forward their side of the story and set the record straight.

This is often a favourite reason for politicians to write their memoirs, particularly once they are out of office and are no longer constrained by being in government.

Example:

Former US President Richard Nixon gives a detailed account of the events surrounding Watergate from his perspective, and his contention that he never authorized the break-in at the Democratic Headquarters, in his *Memoirs of Richard Nixon*.

Tit for tat

If you feel that another writer has written about events which concern you and which appear to cast you in an unfavourable light then putting your side of the story may redress the balance.

Fame

We live in a culture which lauds celebrity, but as quickly as a celebrity is built up then the media tries to bring them down. If fame is your only goal, then be aware of the downside.

Kiss and tell

Depending on who is being kissed and who is doing the telling, this is a way to become a celebrity and make money. But be warned, like writing to be famous, it can backfire and you might get sued.

What kind you want to write

Life stories can be roughly divided into:

- full life story to date
- a defined period within a life
- a story based on themes or topics
- genres.

Full life story

Unless the writer is still scribbling on their deathbed, this is unlikely to cover their whole life from start to finish – although it is not unknown for someone else to finish a life story.

However, full life stories do cover the whole of the writer's life from their birth to the date when they finish writing it. Sometimes they write second or even third volumes to keep bringing their life up to date.

A defined period within a life

For many writers there will be a special period in their life which stands out and which they want to share with other people. This could cover several years or decades or could be as short as one momentous day.

This will probably strike a chord with many older readers who find that memories of early times are starting to come flooding back and who want to describe what their childhood was like.

Other special periods could include:

- school years
- teenage years
- sports career
- marriage
- bringing up a family
- starting a new life

- living abroad
- coping with divorce or losing a partner
- coping with redundancy
- a turning point.

A story based on themes or topics

Basing your life story on themes or topics not only provides an interesting framework on which to hang your book, but it can also be a useful way of breaking the writing down into manageable, self-contained pieces which could provide the basis for letters and articles for magazines (see Chapter 06). For example, if you have artistic talents you could base your life story on your paintings or sculptures. If acting is your forte you could base it on your stage appearances. Other themes or topics can include:

- family members
- friends
- major family events
- jobs
- houses lived in
- holidays
- special moments
- decisions or turning points
- voluntary work
- pets owned
- sporting achievements
- hobbies.

Genres

Life stories can also be defined by genre so you may prefer to write your life story by type such as:

- war
- political
- misery memoirs
- travel
- momentous
- adventurous
- sporting

- celebrity
- unusual or glamorous job
- friend or family biographies
- pet biographies
- humorous (see Chapter 11)
- fictionalized (see Chapters 14 and 15).

War

It is not surprising that war memoirs are so numerous. War has a profound effect on everyone who has ever lived through one, whether as a combatant or a civilian. It is a time of heightened emotions and perceptions, and these memories are often indelibly etched on our minds when others have faded away.

Add to this the elements of danger and excitement and all the ingredients are there for a rattling good story.

Although these kinds of memoirs might seem to be the prerogative of generals or members of the Special Forces, your experiences are still important and deserve to be written down.

Political

These are nearly as numerous as war memoirs, because politicians want to get their view of events across to the public. Of course they don't have to be confined to national politics, and if you can give an inside view of local government, which probably has more effect on our lives than central government, it could make interesting reading.

Misery memoirs

The increasing numbers of misery memoirs, or 'mis lits' as they are sometimes known, indicates the cathartic relief obtained from writing about periods of misery and abuse.

In fact, this type of book is proving so popular that book shops now have shelves specifically for these kinds of life stories – and the numbers of publications are growing. Dave Pelzer's *A Child called It,* which was published in the USA in 1995, was one of the first to hit the market. Since then dozens have been written by people both in the USA and the UK giving harrowing accounts of physical and sexual abuse.

Example:

Julie Gregory's book *Sickened: the Memoir of a Munchausen by Proxy Childhood* details growing up in southern Ohio with a mother who beat, starved and deliberately made her ill with unnecessary medicines to gain attention.

Travel

Although these are usually found in the library's travel section rather than under autobiographies, many travel books could also be defined as life stories based on a certain period of the writer's life.

Examples:

Peter Mayles' *A Year in Provence*, which won the 1989 British Book Awards 'Travel Writer of the Year' category, can also be described as a life story about a specific part of his life i.e. the 12 months he and his wife spent renovating a French farmhouse in Provence. Bill Bryson's many travel books such as *A Walk in the Woods* and *Neither Here nor There: Travels in Europe* incorporate some of his life story.

If you have travelled extensively, both here or abroad, your journeys could form the basis of your life story.

Some cookery books also come into this category.

Example:

John Burton Race's *French Leave*, not only includes dozens of recipes, but also describes in detail the year he and his family spent in a farmhouse in south-west France.

If you are a keen cook and have been round the country, round Europe or even round the world collecting recipes, perhaps these could form the background to your life story.

Momentous

Similar to travel writing are those books written by people who have found themselves caught up in momentous situations, but again they could also be described as life stories.

Examples:

Some Other Rainbow by John McCarthy and Jill Morrell describes his being held hostage in Beirut and Jill's campaign to get him freed. In a similar vein is *An American Hostage* by

Micah Garen and Marie-Hélène Carleton. While *Touching the Void* by Joe Simpson, describes his ordeal when he falls down a crevasse, while climbing with Simon Yates in the Andes, and Simon has to cut the rope joining them.

Not all situations have to be as exceptional as those above, but if you have ever found yourself caught up in abnormal circumstances they could form the basis of your life story.

Adventurous

For some people the spice of life is to push themselves to extremes, such as trekking alone to the North Pole, or going where no man has gone before whether in a remote jungle or finding a new cave under the Mendips.

Examples:

High Adventure by Sir Edmund Hilary, which describes the first ascent of Everest or *Mad, Bad, and Dangerous to Know* by Ranulph Fiennes, an explorer who has lived life on the edge. American author Mary Morris writes about more gentle adventures in her book *The River Queen*, which describes her voyage down the Mississippi in search of her father's childhood places.

Again, your adventure need not be as extreme as conquering Everest or travelling to the Poles, but if for example you had a fear of heights but took up parachute jumping to overcome it then this could form the basis of your life story.

Sporting

Not everyone can be a John McEnroe or Tanni Grey-Thompson, but if you have achieved sporting success then there will be many who would like to read about it, particularly if you have overcome difficulties to achieve that success.

Celebrity

You don't have to be a celebrity to write a best-selling book, it is possible to be famous by association.

Examples:

Paul Burrell, who wrote *A Royal Duty*, is famous for being a butler to the late Diana, Princess of Wales.

New Jersey-born Jancee Dunn who wrote for *Rolling Stone* magazine for many years, alternates chapters about herself with chapters about interviewing the rich and famous such as Dolly Parton in her book *But Enough about Me*.

If you have had an association with someone in the public eye then this could form the basis of your life story.

Unusual or glamorous job

We are all curious about what goes on behind the scenes so there is always an interest in the life stories of people who have had an extraordinary career, whether as a top model, scientist or wife of a diplomat.

Examples:

Open Secret: the autobiography of the former Director-General of MI5, by Stella Rimmington reveals how an ordinary girl became the first woman Director-General of MI5 after being recruited in India when her husband had a job with the British High Commission in New Dehli.

While, *My Spy: Memoir of a CIA Wife* by Bina Cady Kiyonaga, reveals what it is like having to lie about her husband's job as well as coping with the demands placed on a case officer's family.

Even if you don't think your job is as interesting, unusual or glamorous as running MI5 or fielding curious questions at dinner parties, other people may think it is and again it could form the basis of your life story.

Friend or family biographies

These are usually written about people who have had a great influence on the author's life and mean a lot to them. Although essentially biographical they also include part or all of the life of the person writing them.

Examples:

Mitch Albom's *Tuesdays with Morrie* is an account of his visits to his old college tutor, Morrie Schwartz, who, although dying from amyotrophic lateral sclerosis (ALS), passes on his lessons on how to live. It also reveals a lot about the author's life.

For businesswoman, Mary Lucas, it was a means of preserving her father's memory and passing on his words of wisdom.

Case study

I wrote *Lunchmeat & Life Lessons: Sharing a Butcher's Wisdom* as a catharsis during a very difficult time in my life: grieving the death of my father, John Bichelmeyer, who was the local butcher in our small Kansas town. Writing became my way of memorializing the smartest man I ever knew, a father who imparted lasting life lessons to all ten of his children... yet a man with only an eighth grade education.

Dad always had a way of making each one of us feel special. He recognized our individual needs and talents and brought out the best in each of us. I'm proud that I earned my B.D. – which stands for Butcher's Daughter – by spending hours at the family table, listening to my father's stories about how he achieved success by making deep connections with the people around him.

After Dad passed away, I was afraid that all his wonderful bits of wisdom would be lost. I began to write my book as a gift for my family and myself. All my life I listened to his stories and took them to heart. I thought that by writing them down and framing them within my own story I could help inspire others.

Writing this book has allowed me to keep my father's memory alive in ways I could never have imagined. His enduring influence, his wit and wisdom, is now felt by thousands of people that never even met him.

For his headstone, all of his surviving children chose the following words for his epitaph: 'To live in hearts we leave behind means not to die.'

We could never have imagined the continued impact of this heartfelt message to heaven, as The Butcher's Wisdom continues to positively inspire readers. I truly feel my dad's presence each day because of the interest this little book has created around the globe.

Mary Lucas

Pet biographies

Although these are written about the life of a special pet, the owner's life story, or a section of it, is inevitably incorporated.

Examples:

John Grogan's *Marley and Me*, as well as describing Marley's antics also relates the family's life story during that period.

Gavin Maxwell's *Ring of Bright Water* is an autobiographical account of bringing a smooth-coated otter home from Iraq to raise it in Scotland. Doreen Tovey's series of books about Siamese cats also chart her life from 1957.

If you are uncertain what form your life story should take then it is well worth while reading as many different kinds of autobiography as possible because this will not only help you define the type of life story you want to write, but it will also help you find your writing style.

It is likely you already have one or more on your bookshelves. If not libraries are usually well stocked with autobiographies and memoirs. Another good hunting ground is charity shops which nearly always have one or more. If you are after a specific book **www.amazon.co.uk,** or in the USA **www.amazon.com,** are good places to look for both new and second-hand ones.

Who you are writing for

Knowing who you are writing for will have an influence on how you write and what you include. The main groups are:

- family and friends
- yourself
- the public
- posterity.

Family and friends

This is one of the most common reasons, particularly among older people. It is said that our children are not particularly interested in our past, but our grandchildren, for whom it is an alien country, will be fascinated.

If you are aiming at your grandchildren then one of the first things they will want to know is what life was like when you were young – even if they can't really believe you ever were young.

Just because you are writing for people who know you, and some of the circumstances of your life, you still need to fill in all the details. Remember, your book could well be passed down to future generations and they won't know that you used to live in a two-up, two-down cottage with outside loo, or that Uncle George was a family friend not a relation, unless you say so.

Even details which you don't consider important such as the fragility of the old gas mantles or using a mangle to wring out the washing will fascinate future generations.

Example:

The late Arthur Westcott was clear who he was writing his memories down for in 1991.

My Dear Granddaughters,

Now here are the memories of my schooldays as promised you a few years ago and I hope you will find them interesting although they lack any form of sensationalism, neither are they in chronological order and the desultory manner in which they are written arises from the fact that as some struck a chord in my memory, I penned them forthwith. It is as if I put all the incidents in a sack, then turned them out in a heap and picked one at random!

But in recalling them, I seem to have lived again those halcyon days leaving a warm nostalgic afterglow!

Sadly, all the schoolmates involved in these memories are now no more and in the words of the Prophet Elijah;

'I, even I only am left.'

Your affectionate grandpa

Arthur James Westcott.

From Arthur Westcott's book, *Arthur's Village*

Yourself

Even if you never intend to publish your life story or to show it to anyone else, writing them can be beneficial in many other ways as well as being cathartic or therapeutic, such as:

- keeping the brain active
- enjoying doing research
- making sense of the past, particularly family dynamics and divisions
- recalling special occasions
- remembering special achievements
- nostalgia for the past.

Example:

Barack Obama's book *Dreams From My Father* is his search for his identity after hearing that his African father, who walked out on his family when Obama was only two-years-old, had been killed in an accident in Nairobi.

The public

Few of us are going to write life stories which will be snapped up by a publisher and sell thousands of copies in all the major bookstores. But many life stories will appeal to a wider section of the public than immediate family and friends. Libraries and bookshops often have a shelf for locally written volumes.

Example:

Arthur's Village, which recalls Arthur's Somerset childhood between 1900 and 1915, resonates not only with readers who know his area of Somerset well, but also with any who had a country upbringing at the start of the twentieth century.

Posterity

Leaving our memoirs behind us is a way of achieving immortality. Every time our book is read then we are remembered. And why shouldn't you write for posterity: as I said in the introduction everyone has something to contribute to the social history of this country.

Work in progress

My mother decided to write her life story because she wanted to share with her grandchildren and great grandchildren her memories of an idyllic childhood. She also wanted to write it in memory of her two sisters with whom she shared it.

Exercise

Answer these three questions.

Why do you want to write your life story?
What kind do you want to write?
Who are you writing it for?

Whatever your answers to these three main questions are, they are not set in stone. You may start off by deciding to write about a particular section of your life for your own pleasure and find that you are enjoying it so much you write your complete life story and decide to publish it. And that is what the adventure of writing is all about.

Summary

In this chapter you have learnt:

- to define why you want to write your life story
- what type of life story you want to write
- who you are writing it for.

02

making a start

When you write your life story it is the significant and memorable things that seem the obvious ones to include, but your mundane, day-to-day experiences can provide a richer detail, so try to use triggers such as touch or smell to re-awaken those buried memories.

Elizabeth Ashworth, tutor, Writers' News course, 'Making the most of your life experiences'

If you are like most people, once you've made the decision to write your life story then you want to get started straightaway – and nothing could be easier, all you need is a comfortable chair, a pen and some paper. So just sit down and start jotting down your memories.

Getting started

Initially, you will be writing down the memories which most easily spring to mind. However, the brain, like any other part of the body, works better if it is regularly used. So the more time you spend thinking about your past life the more memories will come flooding back.

Making notes

There is nothing to stop you writing your memories down on a notepad or in an exercise book, but memories rarely arrive in chronological order and when you come to start writing your book you will be forever flicking backwards and forwards through the pages trying to find the note that you want.

A better idea is to jot each memory down on three inch × five inch index cards. That way it doesn't matter in what order you write them because when you get to the end you can put together all those cards which relate to each other and they will form a chapter.

I use a similar, cheaper technique where I tear scrap A4 paper into four and have piles in each room, including the bathroom, so that I can jot thoughts down immediately (it's a brilliant way of using junk mail). Then I put them into a folder to look at later. It's surprising how quickly these notes build up – and when the stack is three to four inches high you have the basis of your book.

If you prefer, you can also put your memories straight on to the computer because it is easy to move sections of text around. So put all those thoughts which relate to each other under relevant headings such as 'schools' or 'early childhood memories'. When your document starts to become unwieldy divide the headings into different files.

> **Top tip**
>
> Write down your memories straightaway otherwise you may struggle to remember them again. To my cost I have not always followed this advice.

If it isn't possible or practicable to write down notes yourself, another solution is to use a cassette recorder or battery-operated voice recorder. These are comparatively inexpensive and use standard cassette tapes. You will then need to get someone else to type up your notes or preferably put them on to a computer.

If you are finding it difficult to recall your memories another solution is to get someone to interview you about your life and either record the interview or take notes for you (see Chapter 20 on other forms of publishing).

If they know you well, and what kind of life story you want to write, they will be able to come up with the questions themselves. Otherwise get them to use the list of questions in Chapter 03, 'Writing to a formula'.

Once the interview is recorded you have the choice of having it typed up and turned into a book or downloaded on to CDs instead (see Chapter 20).

Once you have drained your well of memories, the next step is to turn to:

- family and friends
- family archives.

Family and friends

These could be one of your most valuable sources of information and background detail as well as for cross-checking the accuracy of your memories. They will probably also get enthusiastic about your project and help your research by turning out old photo albums and diaries.

Start with those nearest to you and then spread your net wider. While it is better to chat to people face to face, distance sometimes makes it necessary to use the phone or email.

Interviewing on the phone will often produce more information than emailing but you will either have to take notes, record what is being said or ask them to write it all down for you and post it.

Interviewing by email may take longer as the questions and answers fly back and forth through the ether, but this method saves you taking notes, and the information can be saved directly on the computer.

However you record their words, make sure they know what you are going to be doing with the information. No one suddenly wants to find themselves in a book they knew nothing about. And if they are unhappy with what you have written they could sue you.

> **Top tip**
> If you feel it is necessary, get their permission in writing.

Family archives

Unless you have total recall it is unlikely that you will be able to remember everything you want to include, but there could well be other sources of information which will add content and will also trigger further memories. These include:

- diaries
- letters
- old family photos
- family bible
- address books
- school reports
- certificates
- scrapbooks
- quilts
- souvenirs
- jewellery
- medals
- drawers and lofts.

Diaries

Mae West famously said 'Keep a diary, and one day it will keep you.' If you have always kept a detailed daily account of everything you have done, including your thoughts and emotions, you are halfway to writing your life story. Most of us, however, start each New Year full of enthusiasm and then the entries begin to fall off.

But however meagre the number of entries, each could add to the sum total of your life and will help to create a timeline (see below). And it is not just your diaries which will be useful, ask members of the family to check in theirs for information which refers to you.

Letters

Whether they are written to you, from you or about you, these can be a brilliant source of material because not only do they contain solid information about what you were doing at that time, but they may also show your state of mind, the emotions you were feeling and what was going on in the world around you.

Even those between family and friends, whether they include references to you or not, all add more information to the picture you are trying to build up.

Old family photos

While your own photo albums help to trigger memories, the old family photos of past generations may be useful if you intend to add a chapter on the family history.

In the late nineteenth century only the more affluent families had their own camera, but fortunately it was very popular for families to have their photo taken in a commercial studio, even among the less well off. Unfortunately, many of these have neither the name of the subject or the date on which the photo was taken.

It is sometimes possible to establish the date of the photo by the clothes the people were wearing and their hairstyles. There are several books and websites which give examples of photos taken at different periods which may help you to pinpoint the era (see Appendices). Sometimes the name of the studio and even the shape of the photo can also help to date it.

Family bible

These were often used to record births, deaths and marriages so can provide a lot of background detail about the wider family.

Address books

Old address books may reveal a long forgotten relative who may have information. Of course there is a chance they may have moved, but there are websites which help you track people via electoral rolls.

School reports

These will not only remind you of your school days and academic achievements but will probably have the names of all your teachers.

Certificates

Whether they are for cycling proficiency or your PhD they all add to you store of memories and, if dated, could help to put memories into chronological order.

Scrapbooks

These are invaluable because they could contain all kinds of information, including programmes for concerts and shows. 'Baby books' where all the details of a new birth are recorded, and wedding albums also come under this heading.

Quilts

It was popular at one time for family quilts to be made from scraps of material taken from the family's clothes. If you are fortunate enough to have one, the sight of a piece of material from a favourite childhood dress could whisk you back to when you wore it.

Souvenirs

It has long been the custom to bring back holiday souvenirs so it could be worth ransacking the attic where the sight of Goss china from Brighton or the straw donkey from Spain could remind you of a wonderful holiday – or perhaps a totally disastrous one.

Jewellery

Even a few beads can evoke memories of the person who gave the necklace or bracelet and the occasions where you wore them. If the jewellery has been handed down it will remind you of the person who used to own it.

Under this heading I will also include button boxes. Even when a favourite coat or dress as been thrown away many of us still keep the buttons in case they come in useful at sometime.

Medals

Campaign medals will remind you of the various theatres of war you and your relatives served in.

Drawers and lofts

Finally, turning out drawers and lofts can often throw up all kinds of items which may trigger memories.

Using your senses

As well as sight, don't forget we have other useful senses which can also be used to recall memories:

• smell
• hearing
• touch.

Smell

Scents can often be more evocative than sounds or pictures. This is probably due to the fact that the part of the brain which is responsible for registering emotions and long-term memories is closely linked to the part which registers smells.

A sudden smell, such as a special perfume or the scent of a cigar can often produce a rush of memories. But it is also possible to try to deliberately recall certain smells associated with places, people or objects in order to precipitate a memory.

What memories do these smells conjure up for you?

• moth balls
• lavender bags
• seaweed

- hot dogs
- freshly cut grass
- Evening in Paris perfume.

Hearing

Music is also good at bringing back memories. If you still have them, search your old records. It is possible to buy CDs of all the old wartime songs, and some websites allow you to hear clips of these as well as, more chillingly, the genuine sounds of an air raid and a Doodlebug (see Appendices). BBC 7 is also a good place for listening to some of the old radio programmes.

The sound of a cockerel always takes me straight back to the times I stayed with my grandparents and was woken by the crowing of a cockerel. And I still feel the smoothness of the linen sheets and heat from the metal hot water bottle tucked in an old sock to stop it burning me.

Touch

Can you remember what the following felt like and what memories they trigger:

- buttons on liberty bodices
- lino
- sand in your shoes
- woollen bathing costumes
- walking in stiletto heels.

No doubt you will be able to add many more to these lists.

Although the next chapter shows you how to write to a formula, the questions in it can also be used as further memory triggers.

Timeline

Now that you have amassed plenty of information the next step is to create a timeline. This is a useful technique for nailing dates and putting events in the right order.

Take a sheet of A4 paper and draw a line down the centre of it. At the top put your date of birth or the date you intend starting your life story from. At the bottom put in the date your life story will go up to.

On the left-hand side fill in all the dates of the world, national and local events which have occurred during your life such as the beginning and ending of world wars, President Kennedy's assassination, the first moon landing, the first Beatles concert etc. These will help to provide a reference framework. On the right-hand side, fill in the dates of all the memories and events which you have remembered from your own life.

You can also do this on the computer by inserting a table with two columns and as many rows as you need.

Using the information on the left-hand side will help trigger memories of where you were and what you were doing at that time. It will also help to pinpoint the date of your memories. Later, when you come to start writing, the left-hand side information can also add background detail to your memoirs.

Example:

My mother remembered spending an afternoon with her first boyfriend but she couldn't remember whether it was before or after he was posted abroad. However she did remember it was the day that Crystal Palace burned down because they all went to watch. By checking the date of the fire it was easy to see that this was after he came back from his posting and that the date coincided with her twentieth birthday. She was then able to recall that he gave her a watch as a present.

To help you list world events and their dates there are books and websites which specialize in this information. The best known book is *Chronicles of the 20th Century* published by Dorling Kindersley. A list of useful websites can also be found in the appendices.

When the paper becomes too full of dates divide it into quarters, spread the dates out on to four more sheets of paper and start filling in the gaps again.

As a starting point, on the right-hand side fill in all the important dates in your life such as special birthdays, first day at school, university, confirmation, first dance, first date, first day at work, getting engaged, getting married, birth of children, special holidays, first trip abroad etc.

Waiting on the subconscious

Sometimes our memories can prove elusive – the more we try to recall an event or conversation the more our mind refuses to co-operate. If this is the case then try a different approach, tease out memories by letting your subconscious do the work by:

• using relaxation techniques
• soaking in a hot bath and letting your mind wander
• doing something physical like taking a brisk walk.

The secret is not to consciously try to force your mind to recall an event but to wait and see what pops up from your subconscious. But remember to have those cards or scraps of paper handy.

Work in progress

My mother started by writing down memories of her early childhood and the home where she was born. Describing the furniture and fitments in each room brought back memories of family gatherings and little incidents such as how she used to warm her gloves in the range oven before going to school.

She then concentrated on life with her two sisters and her school years. To start with the memories were sketchy, but as she spent more time thinking about the past she was able to fill in more and more details and to recall names and faces she hadn't thought about for more than 80 years.

> **Exercise**
> Write down ten childhood memories, ten school memories, ten dates from your life and ten major events from the same period. Use these to start filling in your timeline.

Summary

In this chapter you have learnt:

• how to use artefacts as triggers
• how to use the senses as triggers
• how to use a timeline.

03

writing to a formula

In this chapter you will learn:
- an easy way of writing a life story
- how to divide up your life
- how to trigger memories.

There is a history in all men's lives.

Shakespeare, Henry IV, Part 2

If you are struggling to write down memories then the simplest way to write your life story is to answer a series of questions.

The ones set out below are not meant to cover every aspect of a person's life, that would be impossible, nor is every question relevant to every reader. However, they do provide a basic framework with which to get started and each reader will undoubtedly add their own questions to the lists.

Write the answer to each question on a separate page of A4 then store the pages in a ring folder. If you are using a computer start a new file for each one. Start with the questions you find easiest to answer to get you going then work your way through the rest.

Top tip

Don't forget you can go back and add more information to the answers as you remember it.

While some questions will probably only elicit short answers, others may run to a page or more. The main thing is to answer each question as fully as possible.

Most lives can be conveniently divided into:

- early childhood
- school days
- work
- religion
- leisure
- courtship and marriage
- having a family
- retirement.

Early childhood

You may not personally remember much about your first two or three years, but you have probably been told where you were born and where you were brought up. By answering the following series of questions about your early childhood you should have enough information for at least your first chapter if not more:

- Where were you born?
- Was it at home or in hospital?
- How was your name chosen?
- Were you named after a relative, someone famous or a character from a book?
- Did you have older brothers and sisters?
- What is the earliest memory you have?
- Was your childhood affluent or poverty stricken, and did this change?

Then think about your house and the place where you lived:

- Did your family have their own house or did you all live with relatives?
- Can you describe each room in your home and its furniture?
- Did it have an inside or outside toilet?
- Did you have your own bedroom or did you have to share?
- Can you describe the area where you lived and the shops?

Now add some more details:

- Who were your friends?
- Where did you play?
- What were your favourite toys, such as a doll, teddy bear or train set?
- What were your favourite clothes?
- What was you favourite food?
- Can you remember a special moment from that period?

Now write down as much as you can remember about your parents during those early years:

- What did they look like?
- Did they both work or was it just your father?
- What was their daily and weekly routine?
- What kind of clothes did they wear?
- What were the funny sayings they used?
- What pet names did they have for you and each other?
- Were they jolly, melancholy, outward going, easy going or shy?
- Did they have any special characteristics or mannerisms?
- What did they like to do for entertainment?
- Were they musical or did they enjoy amateur dramatics?
- What sports did they play?

As well as work and entertainment:

- Did they have any hobbies, if so what were they?
- Did your mother knit, sew, crochet or do any other handicrafts?
- Did your father do woodwork, decorating, house maintenance?
- Did they teach you how to do knitting or woodwork etc.?

Try to recall how you felt about them:

- Can you remember a special moment with them?
- Can you describe your relationship with them?

Then answer the same questions about your grandparents. In addition, add the following information:

- Where did they live?
- What was their home like?
- What was the area where they lived like?
- Did they live a long way away or close by?
- How often did you visit them?
- How did you get there?
- Did you enjoy visiting them or was it a chore?
- What special memories do you have of those visits?

Answer the same questions about aunts, uncles and cousins.

If you have brothers and sisters answer the following questions about each one:

- Are they older or younger than you?
- What did they look like?
- Did you get on well with them?
- What games did you play together?
- What were their favourite activities?
- What were their favourite toys?

Then answer questions relating to special events in your childhood:

- Birthdays: Can you remember any special presents?
- Christmas: Did you spend it at home or with relatives?
- Religious observances: Can you remember your confirmation, first communion or bar mitzvah etc.?
- Empire day, May Day, St George's day, bonfire night, Thanksgiving Day, Independence Day: how did you celebrate these?

- Holidays: Were they in this country or abroad? Did you go camping, caravanning, stay in hotels or guest houses or spend time with relatives?
- Outings: Did you go out for long walks, picnics or car rides?

As well as special events what did you do during the rest of the year:

- Did you go to the cinema, the theatre, the circus or the concert hall?
- Did you have sing-songs around the piano, watch a magic lantern show, listen to the radio, watch TV, play records?
- Did you play board games such as Drafts, Ludo or Monopoly?
- Did you have pets such cats, dogs, birds, goldfish or ponies?
- Did your family have a car or did you use public transport such as buses, trains and the underground?

Few children get through childhood without some accident or illness:

- Did you have any of the major childhood illnesses such as whooping cough, measles etc.?
- Did you break any bones or have other serious injuries and how did they happen?
- Did you have your tonsils or appendix out or any other major operation?
- What was it like in the hospital?
- Were your family allowed to visit?

Finally, how would you describe your childhood:

- Was it happy or sad?
- What were your happiest memories?
- What were your most frightening memories?
- What was your most embarrassing memory?
- Did you have freedom to roam?
- Do you think your childhood was better or worse than that of today's children?

School days

Many people can remember their first day at school as this was probably the first major event in their lives. Answer these questions for your primary and secondary schools:

- What was it called?
- Where was it?
- How did you get there?
- Did you wear a school uniform?
- Can you describe the building, your classroom and the playground?
- Who were your teachers and did you have a favourite one?
- What were school dinners like and did you have them?

School is also about what your learnt and what you played:

- What were your favourite subjects?
- What were your least favourite subjects?
- Did you win a prize for good work?
- What were the punishments and were you punished?
- What sports did you play?
- Who were your school friends?
- What playground games did you play?
- Were there end of year shows for parents? Were you in them?
- What memories of your school days stand out?

Many of the above questions also apply to:

- secondary school days
- university
- training college
- apprenticeship
- night school.

Then write about all the various activities you did outside of school hours:

- Did you belong to Cubs, Brownies, Guides or Scouts?
- What badges did you work for?
- Did you go camping with them?
- Did you go to summer camps?
- Did you have dancing, singing or music lessons?
- What sports did you play?
- What sporting moments stand out for you?
- Did you learn skills such as cooking, sewing and woodwork?
- Did you make collections of stamps, cigarette cards, engine numbers, old coins etc.?
- Did you do part-time work such as paper rounds, helping in a shop, cleaning cars?

Then write about when you became a teenager:

- Did you have sleepovers?
- Did you collect records?
- Did you collect autographs?
- Did you go to jazz clubs?
- Did you go to discos?
- Did you go to pop concerts?
- Did you go to rock festivals?
- Did you join fan clubs?
- Did you go youth hostelling?
- Did you go backpacking?

Can you remember your first:

- girlfriend or boyfriend?
- date and where you went?
- kiss?
- radio?
- television?
- telephone?
- bicycle?
- motorbike?
- car?
- record player?
- record or CD?
- vote, in both local and national elections?

How did you celebrate:

- your 18th birthday?
- your 21st birthday?
- passing your exams?
- getting qualified for your job?
- passing a driving test?

Work

Like school, going into full-time employment for the first time is another major milestone.

Write down all you can remember about your first job/your first day at work

- Did you have to wear a uniform?
- Did you have to clock on?
- Were there any moments when things went wrong?
- Were you called in to see the boss?
- What were your successes?
- Were you promoted?
- Were you made redundant?

Of course many people work for themselves and start their own businesses:

- Did you have your own business?
- How many people did you employ?
- Was your business successful?

Religion

Religion plays a large part in many people's lives:

- Where did you go to worship?
- When were you introduced into full membership of your place of worship such as confirmation?
- Which person had the most influence on you spiritually?
- How has your religion influenced your life?
- Even if you do not believe in a specific religion what spiritual values to you believe in?

Leisure

Leisure time is also an important part of everyone's life:

- Did you go dances, concerts, the theatre?
- What was the dance craze at the time: foxtrot, jitterbug, jive, twist or disco?
- Did you buy records or CDs?
- Who were the popular singers: Mario Lanza, Frank Sinatra, Elvis Presley, The Beatles, The Monkees, Take That?
- Did you go to the cinema? What films made the most impression on you?
- Did you go to plays?
- What play made the most impression on you?

- Did you go to concerts?
- What piece of music made the most impression on you?
- Were you a Teddy boy, hippie, punk or mod?

On the fashion front what did you wear:

- flapper style?
- Oxford bags?
- the New Look?
- the sack dress?
- kipper ties?
- drape suits?
- winklepickers?
- the miniskirt?
- flares?
- bell bottoms?
- leg warmers?

What hairstyles were fashionable? Did you have:

- a shingle?
- pony tail?
- crew cut?
- beehive?
- bubble cut?
- shaggy perm?
- beatle cut?
- bouffant?
- D.A.?
- bob?

Courtship and marriage

This can also be one of the major events of many people's lives:

- Did you marry your first love?
- If not who else did you go out with?
- Why did you break up?
- Where did you meet your partner-to-be?
- Who introduced you?
- Was it love at first sight?

Getting engaged is a special day:

- How long were you going out before you got engaged?
- Where did the proposal take place?
- Was it romantic, surprising or unusual?
- What was the engagement ring like?
- How long was the engagement?
- Do your remember first meeting your future in-laws?
- Do your remember taking your loved-one home to meet your parents?
- Were both sets of parents in favour of your marriage or did you marry against their wishes?

The wedding day:

- What day did you get married?
- Where did you get married – church, register office or a licensed venue?
- What did you wear? What did your other half wear?
- Who was the best man and who were the bridesmaids?
- What hymns did you have?
- Were you nervous?
- Who caught the bride's bouquet?
- Where was the wedding reception?
- Were there any disasters?

Homes

The first home after getting married is special:

- Did you have to live with your parents or in-laws?
- Did you move into a home of your own?
- What was your first home: a house, flat, caravan, mobile home?
- Where was it?
- Can you describe the rooms?
- Did it have a garden?
- What furniture were you able to buy?
- Did you save up for furniture or buy on hire purchase?
- Which item of furniture or ornament meant the most to you?

While some of us stay put and rarely leave the area we were born in, others for various reasons have moved around the country and even around the world. If this has been your experience:

- Make a list of all the houses you have lived in.
- Describe where they were and how long you lived in each one.
- Explain why you had to move.
- Write down something special or striking about each one.

Having a family

Memories come full circle at this point as you recall when and where your children were born and their passage through life and then compare it with your own. Work through the same lists of questions for early childhood. In addition answer:

- Can you remember how you felt when you first held them in your arms?
- How did you feel when they went to school, went to college and left home?
- Do your children still live with you?
- Is this because they are too young to leave home or can't afford to?
- How did you cope with their teenage years?
- Do you have a good relationship with them?
- If they have left home do they live nearby or a long way away?
- How often do you see them?
- Is this often enough or not enough?
- How do you feel about your children?
- Is there any piece of advice you wished you'd given them?

If you have grandchildren answer the same questions as for your children. In addition answer:

- What gives you the most pleasure about having grandchildren?
- Do you think grandparents and grandchildren have a special relationship?
- No matter how much you love them do you enjoy handing them back?

Retirement

This is the time for pursuing those long held ambitions. Since retiring have you:

- done more travelling either at home or abroad?
- taken up voluntary work?
- taken up new hobbies?
- moved to a smaller house or into sheltered accommodation?
- moved to a new area?
- moved to be nearer family?
- overcome illness or injury?
- lost a partner or loved one?
- re-married?
- had to cope with bereavement?

Friends

While we may not be able to choose our families we can choose our friends and they play a major part in our lives. Although there were questions about friends in the earlier sections it might be helpful to think about them in more depth.

- Who were your friends at work, later in life, in retirement?
- Have you kept the same friends throughout life?
- Who do you still keep in touch with?
- Who have you lost touch with?
- Who would you like to make contact with?
- What do they mean to you?
- What special memories do you have of them?

Answer the same questions about your neighbours.

Being part of a community

Few people are entirely isolated from their local and wider community and this does have an effect on our lives as well as shaping who we are.

- Were you politically active either nationally or locally?
- Did you stand for local government?
- Did you belong to a trade union?
- Did you belong to a chamber of trade or other businessmen's group?

- Have you changed your political views over the years?
- Have you belonged to any clubs, groups or societies?
- Have you held any office in them?
- Have you fundraised for any charities or other good causes?

Hindsight

Writing a life story gives the opportunity to look back with the benefit of hindsight and consider what might have been, or whether you should have gone down a different route. Putting these reflections into your life story will help to round it out.

Unless it is too hurtful, try to include the downside of life as well as happier moments because both have made you who you are.

- What were the happiest times of your life?
- What were the saddest times of your life?
- What were the loneliest times of your life?
- Are you happier now than when you were young?
- Do you think your generation is happier than younger generations?
- If you could turn the clock back what would you change?
- What would you do differently?
- Did you always take the right decisions?
- Do you have any regrets about any of your actions?
- Do you have regrets over not taking certain actions?

World War II

Although perhaps not so relevant to younger readers, the years between 1940 and 1945 had a profound effect on all who lived through them. And because this was a time of heightened emotions, most people have very clear memories of that period.

It is therefore not surprising that a sizeable proportion of life stories concentrate on the writers' experiences serving in the armed forces during those years.

In the services

- Did you serve in the Army, Navy, Air Force, Marines?
- What ranks did you hold?

- Where did you do basic training?
- Where were you stationed?
- Did you serve abroad?

Home front

The conflict also had an immense effect on those who remained at home. Men and women who were not actively involved with the fighting had to play their part. Did you do war service in:

- the Home Guard?
- the Air Raid Protection Wardens (ARPs)?
- the fire brigade?
- the ambulance service?
- the Women's Land Army?
- the Women's Royal Volunteer Service (WRVS)?
- the munitions factories?
- the mines?

The following questions could also be answered by someone who was a child during the war. What do you remember about:

- air raid warnings?
- the blitz?
- Anderson shelters?
- sheltering in the tube stations?
- siren suits?
- doodlebugs?
- gas masks?
- identity cards?
- being evacuated?
- Workers' Playtime?
- ITMA?
- Music While You Work?

Rationing

The shortages of food and other commodities affected everyone. What are your memories of:

- ration books?
- clothing coupons?
- British restaurants?
- dried eggs?

- whale meat?
- Spam?
- utility furniture?

Celebrations

Celebrations were few and far between during the war years, but plenty of people did get married and had weddings to remember despite the restrictions on clothes and food.

- Did you get married during the war?
- What did you wear?
- How did you find enough coupons?
- Did you have a wedding breakfast?
- Did you have a honeymoon?

Also consider where you were and how you celebrated:

- V.E. Day on 8 May 1945
- V.J. Day on 15 August 1945
- the return of loved ones.

After the war

Once the victory celebrations were over a period of austerity set in and even the weather was bad.

Do you remember:

- prefabs?
- demob suits?
- fuel shortages?
- ice on the inside of the windows?
- Housewives' Choice?

Other conflicts

Did you serve in:

- Korea?
- Malaya?
- Vietnam?
- the Falklands?
- Iraq?
- Afghanistan?

National service

Between 1945 and 1963 the majority of young men had to do two years' National service in one of the armed forces:

- Can you remember being called up?
- Where were you sent for training?
- Did you serve overseas?
- Did you learn a trade?

Do you remember:

- square bashing?
- Blanco?
- the NAAFI?
- guard duty?
- Forces' Favourites and Jean Metcalfe?

Once you have answered as many questions as you can you should have a fairly complete record of your life in your ring binder. You can then add photos, theatre programmes, bus tickets or other any other documents or illustrations.

There is no need to do anymore if you don't want to – this can be the book of your life story.

Exercise

Answer five questions on your early childhood.

Answer five questions on your relatives.

Answer five questions on your school years.

Summary

In this chapter you have learnt:

- an easy way to write your life story
- an easy way to complete your book
- a way of using questions as triggers.

04

background research

In this chapter you will learn:
- where to find background information
- where to find old photos
- how to record information.

To recall one's schooldays in the early years of this century may not seem very sensational until comparisons are made with those of today, and not only schooldays but the way of life of everybody in the village... The changes which have occurred during the past sixty years or so are simply astounding – they have altered our way of life more so than any which took place in the previous two or three hundred years and for this reason to recall the conditions under which we lived seem worth recording.

Arthur Westcott, author of *Arthur's Village*

Don't be put off by the word 'research': you can do as much or as little as you want – or even none at all if you feel you have amassed enough material.

However, if you do want to try to find out more to add to your stock of information then this chapter will give you some ideas of where to look.

Copyright and plagiarism

Because you will be looking at information produced by other people this is probably a good place to look at these two subjects and what they mean for the writer.

Copyright

The copyright of everything that you read, including information on the Internet as well as in books, belongs to someone, unless it is more than 70 years since the author died. The same applies to all photographs, illustrations and works of art. Even if you have bought the photo or the painting the copyright still belongs to the person who created it.

This means that you can't copy chunks of information from books or Internet sites and put them in your life story without the written consent of the author or creator. The same applies if you want to use any photos, copies of illustrations or pictures. If the author or creator is dead, but the 70 years haven't yet elapsed you will need to get permission from their estate or the owner of the copyright. If you don't do this there is a risk you could be sued.

However, you are allowed to quote a few words under the rule known as 'fair dealing' provided you attribute the quote to the original author or source.

Applying for permission

If you want to quote more than a few words from a source then start by contacting the publisher of the book, magazine or newspaper. Large book publishers will have a special permissions department. Otherwise it is worth ringing to find out who you need to write to so that your letter goes to the right person. Include in your letter the piece you want to quote and when and where it will be quoted.

There will probably be a charge for permission to use quotes, and the cost may depend on whether your book is for family and friends only or whether it will be on sale to the public.

> **Top tip**
> Some book publishers prefer to be contacted by email. Check their website for information on what they require or whether they have specific forms for you to fill in.

The same applies to photographs, illustrations and pictures. If the photo has been taken by a professional studio photographer or newspaper photographer you will need their permission, again there may be a charge. In any event you will need to credit them, such as 'Photo supplied courtesy of the *Evening Planet.*'

It may be possible to use an illustration from very old books which are out of copyright, but if these are in collections such as in reference libraries or county record offices you may still need permission from the library of record office to use it.

If you have a print and the original of a work of art is held in a collection, museum or gallery you will need their permission to use it. Even if you own the original you will need permission from the painter or their estate to use it unless the copyright time has expired.

> **Top tip**
> If in doubt, ask for permission.

Sometimes it isn't easy to find the owner of the copyright and it is not uncommon to find at the front of a book the efforts the author has taken to obtain permission and the promise to remedy any omissions if the owner comes forward.

Plagiarism

Plagiarism is the act of taking other people's words or ideas and using them as if they were your own. If what they are writing about is clearly common knowledge or in the public domain then you can use it but you must write about it in your own words and not just copy or rearrange theirs.

If the information is not in the public domain but is the author's original work or research you will need their permission to use it.

> **Top tip**
> To ensure information is common knowledge or in the public domain try to find two or more different primary sources for it. Always keep records of your sources.

Example:

To write this piece on copyright and plagiarism (words which are in the public domain), I looked at several different sources for definitions of them. I then wrote my definitions in my own words.

As long as you are careful it is unlikely you will breach copyright laws or commit plagiarism, and the good news is that you will own the copyright to everything you have written.

Research

Researching for your memoirs falls into four main categories:

- personal information
- background information
- photos and illustrations
- family tree.

Because researching the family tree is a subject in its own right I will go into that in Chapter 05.

Personal information

When you have spoken to your immediate family and friends and looked at all the family archives for any information about yourself it is time to look further afield. There are several ways of tracking down long-lost relatives, old school friends, work colleagues etc. whom you hope will be able to add to your store of knowledge.

The first port of call is to put their names into a search engine such as Google™ to see if there is any information on the Internet about them or whether they have their own websites where you could get in touch with them.

If that draws a blank then the next step is to try to trace them through:

- specialist websites
- your own website
- the press
- associations
- electoral rolls and old telephone directories.

Specialist websites

One of the largest is Friends Reunited, **www.friendsreunited. co.uk**, where you can search for people by name, or via schools, addresses, armed forces units or work places. There are also message boards on some of the genealogical sites such as **www.rootsweb.ancestry.com**. There are also specialist websites which offer to do searches (see Appendix B).

Your own website

If you already have a website then put a call out on it for friends and relatives to get back in touch. You may also find that relatives you didn't even know existed will contact you.

The press

There are various ways of using the press. Local papers often feature articles or letters from people who want to get in touch with someone. They also like to feature old photographs, such as school photos where readers are asked if they can identify the faces. If you no longer live in the area, or if the person you want to get in touch with has moved, find which local paper you need to contact via the Internet or by checking in the *Writers' and Artists' Yearbook*.

National papers may not be quite so interested in this kind of story, but you could always take a paid advert.

Saga Magazine has a special column for subscribers where you can pay to advertise a request for help in contacting people.

Yours magazine also has a section where readers can ask for help in finding people.

Associations

Under this heading comes:

Old school associations: Contact the school for details or check out their website.

Armed services associations such as RAFA, **www.rafa.org.uk**. See Appendices for other sites. Or try your local council which should have a list of local organizations.

Royal British Legion: Local branches may be listed in the telephone directory or look on the website **www.britishlegion.org.uk**.

Electoral rolls and telephone directories

Some of these are available to look at online via specialist websites. There is a charge for this service (see Appendix B).

To search for updated addresses or phone numbers in the USA try **http://people.yahoo.com/**.

Background information

This is a wide category and could include information as varied as world events, the history of a village, the weather on a certain date or when the local railway line closed.

To avoid mistakes always try to obtain the information from primary sources if possible. Primary sources are the originals such as a diary, a document, a census form or a letter. These have either been written by the person concerned or were written about them at the time. Secondary sources are reports about people and events, such as newspaper stories or books, which were written later, sometimes many years later.

There are various sources for obtaining information:

- the Internet
- libraries
- public record offices
- newspapers and magazines
- local history societies.

The Internet

A lot of the research can be done on the Internet and this certainly saves time and money travelling around the country. If you don't have access to the Internet yourself ask a member of the family if they can help, or use the Internet facilities which are available in Internet cafes or most libraries. Some libraries pay to subscribe to specialist sites, such as the Oxford Reference websites, which you can access for free at the library. Some of them may also be accessible from your home computer, but you will need to obtain a pin number from your library.

One of the simplest ways of researching information on the Internet is to put the subject or year you are interested in into a search engine such as Google™ (**www.google.com**) and Yahoo!® (**www.yahoo.com**) and follow the links. Because each engine searches for information in a slightly different way it is worth trying more than one.

For a more comprehensive search use engines which search other search engines, like Ask Jeeves™ (**www.askjeeves.co.uk**) or All Search Engines (**http://allsearchengines.com**).

One site which nearly always comes up on search engines is Wikipedia. Claimed to be the largest multinational free-content encyclopaedia in the world, the information on Wikipedia is uploaded by volunteers from around the world and it is constantly growing.

But be aware, information on the Internet has been uploaded by all kinds of people. Some of them undoubtedly will have expert knowledge and a genuine reason for making it available to everyone. Others may think what they are saying is accurate, but may have got it wrong. A few may be deliberately putting out erroneous facts.

War and armed forces information

The BBC has an excellent website **www.bbc.co.uk/ ww2peopleswar/**, which has a timeline of all the major events which occurred during World War II as well as 47,000 personal stories and 15,000 images. There are also other sites devoted to this period (see Appendices). For further information on how to access information about members of the armed forces see Chapter 05 on researching family history.

Libraries

History books, local, national and international, will give you background information as will other life stories and biographies. Even fictional books can sometimes fill in the gaps if the author has researched their subject.

For more detailed research you will need to go to a central reference library which may have information on clubs, groups and societies as well as a larger collection of local history books.

It is worthwhile ringing the librarian first to see if they hold the information you are looking for. You may also need to book a seat as space is limited. When you arrive you will probably be asked for identification. You will only be able to use pencils for copying notes, but there should be photocopying facilities. If you have a digital camera, ask if you can take photographs of documents to save you writing out the information on site.

Public record offices

Every county has a public record office housing thousands of books and old documents. These could include church registers, parish council minutes, old court records, old maps and history books of the area, as well as collections of family documents, diaries, postcards, agricultural records etc.

Many have put their catalogues online so that it is possible to see what information is held there before visiting.

As with reference libraries, there is usually limited space so it is advisable to book in advance. Checking the online catalogue in advance and noting down the reference numbers of the documents you need will also save time when you get there. If the archivists have time they might be willing to get out some documents ready for when you arrive so give them the reference number(s) when you book your seat.

As with libraries you are only allowed to use pencils to take notes, but there will be photocopying facilities, and again ask if you can use your camera.

Newspapers and magazines

Old copies of newspapers can be worth their weight in gold when it comes to background information. As well as carrying news stories of the day, they may also included old adverts to trigger the memory, birth, marriage and death announcements and what the weather was like.

The major archive for magazines and newspapers is the British Library at Colindale, North London, which holds a vast collection. You can check their catalogue online on their website **www.bl.uk/collections/newspapers.**

Some papers such as the *Daily Telegraph* have their own online archive which allows you to look at stories from the past few years. And there is an excellent site for *The London Illustrated News* dating from 1842, **www.iln.org.uk/.**

The US website **www.ancestry.com** allows access to hundreds of newspapers and periodicals online, but there is a charge.

Local newspapers often hold back copies for the past year or two which can be viewed at their offices. Older copies are often microfilmed and can be viewed at the reference library.

There are also various companies which sell original copies of newspapers, or books containing copies of newsworthy stories (see Appendices). It is also possible to buy CDs of old news reels, wartime songs and radio broadcasts.

The *Soldier* magazine website **www.soldiermagazine.co.uk/flashback/index.htm** also has an archive feature where you can look at articles dating back to 1955. Old copies of the *Armed Forces* magazine are often available on eBay.

Local history societies

Most areas have a local history society or something similar. Some of them produce books or magazines with stories or anecdotes from the past. One way of finding them on the Internet is to put the name of the area you are interested in into a search engine. There is also a website **www.local-history.co.uk/Groups/,** which contains contact details of some of them.

If this draws a blank try contacting your district or parish council, library or tourist information centre – again find them on the Internet – and ask for details of any history groups.

Other

The BBC has an extensive archive of information relating to broadcasting going back to 1922. And don't forget museums, which not only may have artefacts which could trigger memories, but also background information about the area and local people.

Photos and illustrations

Photos of the family and places where you lived not only help to jog memories, but can also be used to illustrate your life story should you decide to publish it.

The first port of call is obviously the family album, but there are other places to look as well.

Internet sites

There are several sites which hold vast collections of old photographs and postcards – of both people and places (see Appendix B). On some sites they are available to buy, on other sites they are available to download for personal use.

Top tip

Always check the conditions of use on each site to avoid breaking copyright laws.

It is also worth looking on the eBay website as there are plenty of sellers with old postcards which may include some of where you were born and brought up.

There are also websites which hold items such as old theatre programmes, which are available to buy (see Appendix B).

Books

Old books may contain useful illustrations of places or areas where you used to live.

Top tip

If you want to copy a photograph or illustration from a book it is better to use a digital camera rather than a photocopier. This is because it is difficult to get a book completely flat in a photocopier and the picture becomes distorted. Set the camera to 'close up' and if the book has shiny pages turn off the flash otherwise you will get a reflection of the flash in your picture.

Estate agents

It is worth looking on estate agents' details to see if they are selling your former home or one which looks similar. If there is a photograph contact them to ask if you could use it in your book. You should also contact the current owner of the house to check that they are happy with this.

Professional photographers

If it is too far for you to travel to the place you want photographed then it might be worthwhile contacting a professional photographer to take the pictures for you. Names can be found on the British Institute of Professional Photography website **www.bipp.com** or The Royal Photographic Society website **www.rps.org**.

For US photographers go to **www.dmoz.org**, click on 'arts' and then on 'photography'.

Handling data

By now you have probably started to collect a sizeable amount of information and if it is not to overwhelm you it is essential to set up some form of filing system to keep it all under control. This doesn't need to involve expensive equipment: used A4 envelopes and cardboard boxes are fine for storing handwritten notes, photos and books.

> **Top tip**
> Mark on the outside of each envelope what it contains and keep an index – this saves endless hunts for information.

If you use a computer not only will you be inputting your notes but also downloading useful information from the Internet. Again, to save needless searching you will need to set up a filing system with an index and the name of the folder each piece of information is stored in. Make sure you include in each folder the name of the website and the name of the person who owns the copyright to it.

Backups

Once you have amassed all this information you don't want to lose it if your computer crashes or is damaged in any way so regularly download it on to CDs, memory sticks (sometimes called flash drives), USB cards, separate hard drives or floppy disks, and store them somewhere safe, away from the computer.

It is possible to have two hard drives on your computer and save information on both as a backup, but it is more useful to have portable backups because they can be used on another computer if yours has crashed.

There are also Internet companies which, for a fee, will store information on their computers. Some also offer a recovery service if you have accidentally deleted an important file (see Appendices).

> **Top tip**
>
> Get into the habit of backing up your work on a regular basis: either daily or every 1,000 words.

Work in progress

To find background information for my mother's life story I put the name of the village where she was born into Google™. Among the many sites which came up was the parish council. That site had links to village organizations, including the local history society. The local history site had plenty of interesting information including details of a book written about the history of the village. We obtained a copy of the book, which not only brought back many memories for my mother, but also had plenty of background information.

Exercise

Find out background information using either the library or the Internet.

Track down your nearest local history society.

Set up a filing system.

Summary

In this chapter you have learnt:

- how to avoid breaking copyright
- how to research background information
- how to find illustrations.

05

researching the family tree

If you'd like to trace your family tree, the first thing is to talk to your living relatives. Next you need some concrete evidence to find out the names and dates of your ancestors; using the birth, marriage and death records, plus the censuses, you can begin to build your family tree. Why not sign up to one of the key family history websites, which will let you find these records online? Your journey into the past will have begun, and you'll be amazed at the historical records that you'll discover on the way to help.

Helen Tovey, Editor *of Family Tree Magazine*

Interest in researching family histories has been given a boost by various television programmes where well-known personalities discover their roots – sometimes with unexpected results. Even if you do not intend including your family history in your life story you may find it interesting and helpful to know where you have come from.

Of course, you may find yourself connected to rich, famous, titled or infamous families. But for most of us the research will probably reveal some unknown relatives, a few skeletons in the cupboard, a few tragedies and – most surprisingly – how much our forbears moved around the country.

Example:

My mother was born in Surrey and thought that was where her family roots were. When she moved to Cheddar in Somerset she immediately felt at home. Tracing her family tree revealed why – her great, great grandmother was born in Axbridge, just a mile or so away from Cheddar.

In fact that is another one of the surprises of family research: because there is now so much information publicly available we probably know more about our ancestors than their own children did.

Example:

I remember my Grannie telling me how she watched the funeral procession of Queen Victoria. As a child I was vaguely interested but never thought how she happened to be in London at the time. However, researching the family tree I found on the 1901 census that she and her sister were both working as maids in a house in Knightsbridge. It is likely that their employers gave all the staff some time off to watch such a momentous occasion. Until my research my mother had no idea that her mother had worked in London before getting married.

Researching the family tree can become a lifelong study involving visits to archives around the country as you try to go further and further back in time. However, for the purposes of adding a chapter to your book about your immediate ancestors you should be able to find most of the information sitting at a computer, visiting local libraries or applying for documents through the post.

It is possible that other people are also looking for the same family members that you are, so before plunging into your research it is worth checking to see what, if anything, has already been discovered. There are several websites (see Appendices) where you can find out who else is collecting information on your family. You can also post your results for others to see and perhaps share information.

> **Top tip**
>
> The US website **www.ancestry.com** has a database called OneWorldTree, click on it, fill in the name you are researching and specify the country, and up will come information which has been downloaded from other family trees. (At the time of writing this facility was not available on **www.ancestry.co.uk**.)

There are three main sources for tracing information about your ancestors:

- birth, marriage and death certificates
- censuses
- documents.

Birth, marriage and death certificates

Try to collect as many of these as possible as the information on them will go a long way to getting you started on your family tree. They may also provide you with the information needed to start looking on the censuses.

> **Top tip**
>
> Bear in mind that mistakes are made on documents, sometimes due to clerical errors and sometimes because people couldn't remember accurately their age, date of birth or where they were born.

Birth certificate

A full certificate will give the following information:

- Name of child: This will not only give all the child's forenames, but also the correct order. People are sometimes known by their second name or even a completely different name, which makes it extremely difficult to trace them in a census.
- Date of birth: This is essential when trying to work out which John Smith in the census is the correct person. It is also a major piece of information to add to your family tree.
- Where born: Again this helps to confirm you have found the right relative in the censuses. It also gives an indication of how much the family moved around the country and whether each child was born in a different locality.
- Name of father: This information enables you to move back a generation and find them on an earlier census.
- Father's occupation: As well as helping to identify that you have found the right relative on the census forms, it can also show how people changed jobs or moved from being an employee to having their own business.
- Name of mother including maiden name: The mother's first name is a major clue when trying to establish that you have found the correct family, but even more important is her maiden name because that enables you to start tracing the female line.
- Date of registration: If greatly different from date of birth it gives an indication of how difficult it was to register a birth.

Other information which can be gleaned is whether it is the original or a copy. If it is a copy then the date of the copy and the reason it was supplied could give a clue as to what the person was doing at that time or what was happening.

Example:

On my grandfather's copy of his birth certificate it says it has been issued for the purposes of 'Widows, Orphans and Old Age Contributory Pensions Acts' and it is dated 5 September 1946. In that year the Labour Government passed The National Insurance Act which brought in the welfare state. Perhaps he needed this certificate to claim his old age pension.

If a birth was illegitimate the birth certificate might also give the name of the father.

Marriage certificate

This will give the following information:

- Date of marriage: This is a major date to add to your family tree.
- Where it took place: Again this helps to establish whether families moved around or stayed in the same place.
- Full names of the couple and ages: Like the birth certificate knowing the correct names helps to trace relatives and their ages can be cross-referenced against the year they were said to be born.
- Status: This may show if either had been married before and help you trace former partners and children.
- Occupation: Knowing an occupation helps to establish that you have found the right relative on the census forms.
- Where living at time of marriage: This fills in details of where the groom was living at the time, which might be different from where his family was living.
- Name of both fathers: The name of the bride's father enables you to research the bride's family tree.
- Occupation of both fathers: Again this will help confirm whether you have found the right person on the census form – be aware, however, that mistakes can be made.

Example:

On my in-laws' marriage certificate the registrar wrote the groom's first names instead of the bride's father's first names. This would have caused endless confusion if we had been relying on that document to track down my mother-in-law's father on the census forms. It also looks as if the registrar put the wrong address in for the bride.

Death certificate

This gives the following information:

- Date of death: This is another important date to add to the family tree.
- Where: This might give information about the circumstances in which your relative was living, such as with relatives. The certificate also shows where they died, either at home or in hospital.
- Name and age of deceased: This is useful for cross-referencing with other documents and census forms.

- Address: Again useful for cross-referencing with other documents.
- Occupation: Tells us whether the deceased was still working or retired. Also useful for cross-referencing with other documents.
- Cause of death: This not only tells us the kind of diseases which were prevalent at the time but could indicate if certain occupations were hazardous.
- Informant: This is the person who registered the death, usually a relative. This can sometimes give you a clue to an unknown family member.

Register offices

If you don't have any certificates or not enough to start creating the family tree, then it is possible to buy copies going back as far as 1837. The two main sources of supply are:

- local register offices
- the General Register Office (GRO), London.

Local register offices

These offices will be able to provide certificates provided the event took place in the area covered by the office.

It is essential to ring them first because the level of information required, the time it takes to issue the certificate and the fees charged, vary from office to office. You can find their number in the telephone directory or go to the GRO website **www.gro.gov.uk**, find the information box for 'Register Offices' and follow the links until you find the right address and phone number.

For birth and death certificates you may only need the name, the year and the quarter, and the place for the event. For marriage certificates far more detail is required to trace them.

> **Top tip**
> Local Register Offices can't trace certificates from the Registrar General's index reference (see overleaf).

The General Register Office

To buy certificates from the GRO you will either need the full details of the event or the Registrar General index reference.

The State started registering births, marriages and deaths in 1837 and by and large nearly everyone since then has had these major moments of their life recorded for posterity. The information was collected locally and every three months the local superintendents sent the Registrar General certified copies.

This information was collated in three separate indexes: birth, marriage and death. Up until 1984 the information was entered in quarters: that is January to March, April to June, July to September and October to December. After that date they were entered annually.

The entries are in alphabetical order by surname followed by forenames. The index also gives the registration district, volume number and page number, and this is the information which is referred to as the index reference.

A lot of the indexes can be accessed online. Volunteers are currently transcribing the information which can be accessed for nothing on **www.freebmd.org.uk** and more is being added on a regular basis.

> **Top tip**
> If you can't find the information you want try again a few weeks later in case it has been added recently.

There are also several other websites where you can access this information, but there is usually a charge (see Appendices).

The full indexes can be viewed for nothing in The National Archives at Kew, Richmond, Surrey, telephone +44 (0) 20 8876 3444 or see the website **www.nationalarchives.gov.uk**. (The indexes moved here from the Family Record Offices in 2008.)

They can also be viewed in local libraries, but what is held does vary from library to library so it is worth telephoning them first. Even if they don't hold what you want they will be able to point you to a library near you that does.

They are also held at the Church of the Latter Day Saints family history centres. Check on their website **www.lds.org.uk** for details of a centre near you. As these centres are run by volunteers the opening hours will vary so check the times by ringing the Hyde Park Family History Centre on +44 (0) 20 7589 8561.

The indexes will give limited information about the people, but they are useful for cross-referencing with other documents. However their main benefit is to give you the index reference information needed to buy copies of certificates.

Index reference information

If you find the right relative you will need to note the:

- year of the event
- quarter
- name of the district where it took place
- volume number
- page number.

Multiple names

Unfortunately there is often more than one entry in the indexes which could be your relative. If you can't be certain you have the right one you may have to buy more than one certificate.

With the marriage indexes it is often possible to find the other partner by cross-referencing the page and volume number to see who else is listed on the same page or on the pages either side. There are four names on each page and the two people marrying are not necessarily listed next to each other. But if you have a forename for the missing partner this can help to pinpoint them.

Example:

I found my husband's grandfather listed by surname in the marriage index, I then looked to see who else was on the same page by searching the index via the volume and page number. Of the other names listed one had the same forename as his grandmother, which not only showed I had found the right entry for his grandfather, but gave me her surname as well.

Buying certificates

These can be obtained from the General Register Office, website **www.gro.gov.uk**. They can be ordered online via the website, either using the information from the indexes, or by giving the exact details of the event. They can also be ordered by post from GRO, PO Box 2, Southport, Merseyside, PR8 2JD or by phone 0845 603 7788.

> **Top tip**
> Don't forget to order the full birth certificate and not the short one which will not have all the important information on it.

In the USA each state will have its own office for obtaining certificates. Use the **http://genealogy.about.com/library/blvitalus.htm** website, then click on the map for the address and details of where to send for certificates. Birth and Death records can be ordered from **www.vitalrec.com**. There are various websites for searching records (see Appendices) but you have to be a member and there is a charge for joining.

Once you have some information from the certificates you can start drawing the family tree. Various websites allow you to draw your tree online (see Appendices). Otherwise you can create it on your computer or write it out on a large sheet of paper. Once you start researching side branches you may have to draw separate trees for each branch.

Censuses

It is possible to create your family tree from birth, death and marriage certificates, but if you have to pay for those which are missing it gets expensive. Once you have sufficient information from family documents to get you started, it is a cheaper option to do your research via the censuses. For the price of one or two certificates you could pay to look at dozens of different databases and documents.

Censuses have been held every ten years since 1801 (apart from 1941), but they are only available online from 1841 to 1901. However the earlier ones were basically headcounts and would not have much information of interest to researchers.

Each census was taken on one day and they provide a snapshot of where each person was on that date. This can throw up some interesting information such as where people were working and who was visiting whom.

1901 census

The 1901 census was taken on 31 March. It gives the full names of all the people residing at a particular address on that day and their relationship to the head of the household. It also gives their ages at their last birthday, where they were born, their marital status, occupation, their employer if relevant and medical disabilities. Because elderly parents often lived with their children, knowing the relationship of residents can often help to trace the previous generation.

1851–1891 censuses

These give the same information as 1901 and were taken on:

- 1891 – 5 April
- 1881 – 3 April
- 1871 – 2 April
- 1861 – 7 April
- 1851 – 30 March

1841 census

This was taken on 6 June and only contains the address (but often not the number of the house), the name of the residents, their age (rounded down to the nearest five if over 15 years), where born and their occupation.

1911 census

Censuses are not normally made public for a full 100 years, but such has been the demand to access at least some of the information contained in the 1911 one, that the National Archives are considering whether to make some of it available online in 2009.

US censuses

Census information in USA is available from 1790 to 1930. Some of the 1790 census records are missing and most of the 1890 records were destroyed in a fire. The later census records have more information about each individual than the UK census records.

Accessing and utilizing censuses

Although information from the censuses was available to view at the Family Record Centre and is now available at the National Archives at Kew, the big step forward for family history researchers was when the 1901 census was made available online in 2002. So many people wanted to access the information that the site immediately became overwhelmed. The other censuses have been added since then.

The censuses, both in the UK and USA, can be accessed from various websites (see Appendix B). The choice of which site to use is a matter of personal preference – choose the one you find easiest to navigate around, and which offers the best value for money. Quite often they will offer a free trial period. On some sites it's possible to find limited information about a relative for free, but you will have to pay to access the original record to check that you have found the right one.

At the time of writing it is possible to access information from the 1881 UK census for free on **www.familysearch.org**, including the names, ages and occupations of everyone in the household on that day.

> **Top tip**
> You may be able to access all the records held on **www.ancestry.co.uk** for free if your local authority pays a subscription to the site. It is worthwhile checking with your library as this could save you a lot of money.

To trace your family tree through the censuses you need to work backwards from 1901, and to do that you need sufficient information about a relative who was alive in that year and would therefore appear on the census. Once you have pinpointed them it should be possible to trace them or their forebears back through the earlier censuses.

Once you have traced an ancestral line back as far as you can, it is then possible to work forwards following another strand to see what happens to other parts of the family.

Along the way you may find, as I did, relatives you didn't know existed, some minor tragedies and some happy endings.

Top tip

If you are having difficulty in tracing a relative it may be because their surname has been spelt differently. People sometimes changed the way they spelt their name or the census enumerator may have written it down wrongly. So be prepared to look at alternative spellings.

Information needed

If your relative has an unusual surname then you probably only need a name and a date of birth, otherwise you will need the following:

- forenames
- where born
- where living at the time of the census.

The more information you can input into the website the more precise will be the results. But even then you could be faced with two, three or even more possible choices. At this point you may have to pay to see the original forms to see if there is further information to help pinpoint the right relative such as the names and ages of other known siblings or the person's occupation.

Top tip

Other clues are: the same forenames sometimes keep cropping up in families as parents often named their children after themselves and siblings often named their children after their aunts and uncles.

Once you have found the right person, the census form will tell you where they were living at the time of the census although it may not always show the number of the house. This gives an insight in to how people moved around a district or even around the country. It is also possible that their houses still exist.

Example:

We found the address of my mother's great grandmother in Bridgwater and were able to go and see the row of houses where she was brought up. Even though we didn't have the number for the property, we were able to get an idea of how small the two-up, two-down would have been for a family of eight.

It is much easier to track back through the male line because the wife's maiden name is not shown on the census. However, family research is a bit like detective work and there are clues which can be used to track down a wife's maiden name.

Example:

A census I was looking at showed that a sister was visiting the family; as she had a different surname to the wife there were three possibilities: she was the husband's married sister, she was the wife's married sister, or she was the wife's unmarried sister. If the last option was the case I now had the wife's maiden name. I confirmed that by looking for the sister on a previous census, which showed her and the wife living at home with their parents.

Top tip

Not everyone appears on the census, if you can't find them on one try looking on the next earliest one.

Of course it isn't always plain sailing and you may need to approach the search from a different angle. If you can't find a husband try looking for his wife or children instead.

Example:

I could not find one of my husband's grandfathers on the 1901 census even though I had all the information needed to track him down. Then a distant relative of my husband came to visit and we were able to work out that his grandmother and my husband's grandmother had been sisters. This gave us enough information to track down my husband's grandmother on the 1901 census. We then discovered why we had not been able to trace his grandfather – he had changed his forename from Frederick to Frank. As his surname was a common one it would have been like looking for a needle in a haystack without his wife's name to help us.

Searching by addresses

If you know where a family member lived it is possible to access their information by searching for their address rather than by name. At the time of writing this facility was available for 1901, 1891, 1871 and 1861, but it will probably be available for the other dates within a short time.

Searching by address can be used to track down a relative if you have no other information about them other than where they lived, but it will mean looking at page after page of census records until you find them. Realistically it is probably only worth doing this if you can pinpoint the village or area where they lived.

> **Top tip**
> Be aware that not all houses had numbers, many properties have been renumbered and some streets have been renamed.

Documents

There are plenty of other documents which could help to fill in the gaps. The most useful are:

- parish registers
- wills
- military records
- electoral registers.

Parish registers

Baptisms, marriages and burials, which take place in church, are all recorded in the church registers. Although the information may be similar to that recorded in the civil registration documents, it can fill in gaps because not everyone realized that, for instance, they had to register the birth of a child as well as having them baptised.

> **Top tip**
> The date of registration of a birth could be some time after the actual date of birth.

A start has been made on transcribing these parish registers on the Genuki website **www.genuki.org.uk** so it is possible to view some of them online. The site is easy to navigate around: click on 'contents and search', then on 'England page', then on a county, then on 'towns and parishes' and finally select the relevant town or parish. This page will tell you what information is available online and where to find other information.

As more records are being added all the time it is worth looking on a regular basis to see if the ones you are interested in have become available.

Although current parish registers remain in their churches, the older ones can now be found in the local county record office. Some libraries and family history centres also hold copies so it is worthwhile contacting them first if they are nearer to you.

Before going to the county record office, check to see if they have an online catalogue. This will allow you to browse through the documents held and if they have the ones you want you may be able to order them when you make an appointment to visit so that they are ready and waiting for you.

Wills

Not everyone made a will, but those which exist will probably give you an interesting insight into family relationships as well as revealing unknown relatives.

Pre 1858

Wills proved before 1858 from the southern half of England are available online on the National Archive website **www.nationalarchives.gov.uk/familyhistory/wills**. Once you have found the will you are interested in from the index you can pay to download it straight to your computer. At the time of writing the cost was £3.50.

Wills for the northern half of England are held in the Borthwick Institute for Archives **www.york.ac.uk/inst/bihr** which is situated on the University of York campus. You can visit the archive search rooms to look at the indexes.

If you have the date of death, burial or probate you will usually be able to order copies. For full details and the form to fill in, click on 'reprographic services' on their website. Or write to them at Borthwick Institute, University of York, Heslington, Yorks, YO10 5DD, or telephone +44 (0)1904 321166. The institute is also able to carry out research for you but it will cost a minimum of £15 and will go up depending on the amount of time you want them to continue searching.

Post 1858

The index to those proved after 1858 can be viewed on microfiche at the National Archive Kew, but the wills themselves are held by the Court of Probate. You can access them and buy copies at the Probate Search Room, First Avenue House, 42–49 High Holborn, London, WC1V 6NP, telephone +44 (0) 20 7947 7022. You can also order copies by post from Probate Sub-Registry, First Floor, Castle Chambers, Clifford Street, York, YO1 7EA. The website for the Court of Probate is **www.hmcourts-service.gov.uk**, click on 'wills and probate', then in the information box click on 'searches and researches', then on 'guide to obtaining copies of probate records'.

Military records

More and more information about military records is being made available online. The National Archives **www.nationalarchives.gov.uk** is a good place to start. The Imperial War Museum **http://london.iwm.org.uk/** also has plenty of information and links to other sites.

The Commonwealth War Graves Commission keeps records of all those who died in the two world wars. Their 'debt of honour register', which gives information of where servicemen are buried, can be accessed online at **www.cwgc.org**.

The US website **www.militaryindexes.com/** gives links to information from the Revolutionary War to the Vietnam War.

Electoral registers

These can be useful for finding addresses of people. They were produced annually starting in 1832, except for 1916 to 1917 and 1940 to 1944. They are held at the British Library, 96 Euston Road, London, NW1 2DB, telephone +44 (0) 20 7412 7536.

As many of the registers are held off-site you will need to give 48 hours' notice of the ones you want to look at. You will also need identification to obtain a Reader's Ticket.

Major reference libraries may also hold registers for their area. The National Libraries of Scotland and Wales hold the collections for those countries.

Visiting archives

Because at the moment there is still much more information available in the archives than online, a visit to the relevant centres where the documents are held, may be necessary if you get stuck or want to pursue the trail further back. You can also view censuses for nothing rather than having to pay to view online.

As these are busy places you will probably have to book a seat in advance. Take identification with you as it may be required. Usually you are only able to take pencils with you into the archives for making notes, but some may allow you to photograph documents. There may also be facilities for photocopying.

To make the best use of your time make a list before you go of exactly what you intend to look for. Don't be too ambitious, it always takes much longer than you think to do research. It also gets very tiring looking at microfiche through a viewer for long periods. Most documents and microfiche have to be retrieved from the vaults, so be prepared for a wait.

Top tip

Check on their website in advance to see what documents are available and their catalogue number to save time when you arrive. It is worth trying to book one or two documents when you book your seat so that they can be available as soon as you arrive.

Keep notes of everything you find, where it came from and its catalogue number – never rely on remembering information. Keep a list of every document you look at and its catalogue number so that you don't look at the same documents twice.

If you no longer live in the area where you want to search for relatives, or find it difficult to get to the main archives, it often pays to use a professional researcher, who knows exactly where to look, rather than spending time and money on travel.

The National Archive website **www.nationalarchives.gov.uk** has a list of researchers and it is worth checking other archive sites to see if they have similar information.

> **Top tip**
>
> If you are researching old documents held in libraries or county record offices, even though the author has been dead for more than 70 years you may still need permission to use excerpts or illustrations from them. This also applies to original documents such as censuses and indexes which can be accessed on the Internet.

Further help

The information above is sufficient to get you started, but it is only scratching the surface. If you want to undertake a more serious study of your family tree or go back further than three or four generations then it is worthwhile seeking help.

Many libraries have archivists who are able to help and advise. There are also some excellent books, such as *Teach Yourself Tracing Your Family History*, published by Hodder Education, which is packed with useful information, as well as several monthly magazines specializing in family history research.

Lives in context

Local history societies often hold documents of interest for researchers, and many publish regular articles and booklets. These could include information on families who have lived in the area for generations, former occupations, schools etc.

Even if your family is not specifically mentioned in the articles, they will give you an idea of what life was like for your relatives in former times and what they were going through.

Once you have completed your family trees it is worthwhile matching them to what was happening in their locality, in the country and in the wider world because this will give you a better understanding of the times they were living through and what their lives would have been like. This can be done by drawing a timeline to correlate family dates with external events.

Google Earth™

If you can access Google Earth™, this wonderful new tool allows you to zoom in on any area in the world where your relatives once lived, and get a bird's eye view of it. Naturally many places may have undergone considerable changes, but others may look exactly the same.

Work in progress

We had enough information to find family members on the 1901 census. We then traced the lines back as far as the 1841 census, which gave us the earliest date of 1778, when my mother's great, great, grandmother was born.

Exercise

Research information on the free births, marriages and death site.

Check online catalogues for your local record office.

Try to find your relatives on the 1901 census.

Summary

In this chapter you have learnt:

• how to order birth, marriage and death certificates
• how to use the census records
• how to use the archives.

section two

writing

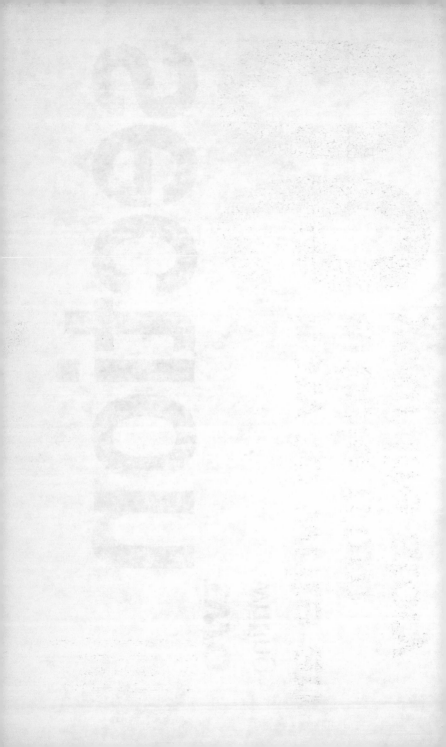

06

how to write an article from your life story

In this chapter you will learn:
- how to write an article
- where to send articles
- how to analyze an article.

Make sure your story suits the magazine and has appeal to their readership. See if they have reader guidelines or else use the features in the magazine as a guide to length and style. Always type your submission. Make your first sentence exciting. Your submission is one of many – make it stand out.

Valery McConnell, Editor of *Yours* magazine

The big moment has come – you have collected all the information and you know what kind of life story you intend to write – all you have to do now is get it down on paper or on the computer.

But if this appears daunting, don't worry, the secret is to break it down into manageable chunks. Rather than thinking about writing the whole book in one go why not consider writing all, or part of it, as a series of articles or letters for publication.

Benefits of writing an article

Producing saleable articles or letters has several benefits:

- It gives you the chance to practise your skills on something shorter than a complete book.
- If you write enough articles you will have a basis for your book.
- If you are hoping to publish your life story it enables you to test the market first, and if successful it provides proof to send to potential publishers.
- It can be financially rewarding.

Outlets

There are several outlets for articles, including:

- general magazines
- real-life story magazines
- newsletters
- history societies
- letters pages.

General and real-life story magazines

Look along the shelves of any newsagents and you will see there are dozens if not hundreds of magazines covering nearly every subject. Some will feature several life story articles and may even invite articles based on specific topics such as 'A childhood memory', or 'Your first day at work'. Others may only include them if the article fits the remit of the magazine such as only accepting articles from people living within the area covered by the magazine (see Appendix B).

Not all magazines take articles by freelance writers, but you can check this by looking at the magazine listings in *The Writer's Handbook* or the *Writers' and Artists' Yearbook*. These books are published annually and can be bought from any good bookshop or borrowed from the public library. I couldn't find an equivalent publication in the USA, but Wikipedia has a comprehensive list on its website, **http://en.wikipedia.org/wiki/Category:American_magazines**, where you can find basic information about each magazine and links that will take you to their websites.

> **Top tip**
> While many top-selling magazines welcome articles, they are often overloaded with submissions so try looking for smaller, niche publications.

Newsletters

Many clubs, groups and societies such as ex-service organizations produce regular newsletters for their members and welcome pieces on members' experiences. In a similar vein so do local councils and churches.

History societies

If your local society produces books, newsletters and other publications, they may well be interested in an article about a section of your life as long as it gives information about the area covered by the society. If you no longer live in the locality which features in your article then try to get in touch with the history society covering that area.

Letters pages

Most magazines have a letters page, and many pay quite well for those that are published. So if you would prefer to start off by writing something shorter than an article why not write a letter. These are generally based on an anecdote or small incidents, and humorous ones are popular.

Types of articles

Look for areas of your life story which can be told as self-contained anecdotes. These can be:

- nostalgic
- life affirming
- memorable
- informative
- humorous.

Nostalgic

As the name suggests these are about things which have happened in the past; perhaps a memorable incident from your childhood or days in one of the armed services. They can be written in a reflective style or tied in to current events by comparing things now with things past.

Life affirming

Perhaps you have overcome specific difficulties or have achieved something amazing such as fostering dozens of children or raising thousands of pounds for charity against the odds.

Memorable

This could be a special event, a turning point in your life, or an unusual experience.

Informative

Use your experience to give help and advice to others. For example, if you have lived abroad explain how you coped with a different language and customs.

Humorous

There is always a market for humorous articles. Look for some small incident which had amusing consequences. A little bit of poetic licence is allowed in the telling. However, they can be more difficult to write.

Writing articles

The skills required for writing articles will stand you in good stead when it comes to writing your complete life story. And while few books are written in the same brief way as newspaper reports, it is still useful to bear in mind the following journalistic principles:

- Make life easy for the reader.
- Make your meaning clear.
- Answer the six questions: Who, What, Why, Where, When and How.

Opening paragraphs

Opening words need to grab the reader's attention as well as setting the tone for the rest of the article. More importantly they need to grab the editor's attention otherwise they may not want the article on the assumption that their readers won't be interested in it either.

Openings can be:

- provocative, intriguing or surprising
- scene-setting or atmospheric
- a question
- humorous
- ironical.

Some writers like to write their opening paragraph first, while others prefer to wait until they have written the article and then decide how best to start it.

Body of the article

If the opening paragraph has been written to attract the reader's attention then the next paragraph may need to show how it connects with the rest of the article. This is called a bridging paragraph and there are three different types:

- Nub: This tells the reader what the article is going to be about.
- Background information: This gives relevant information which the reader needs in advance to understand the article.
- Context: this tells the reader about the circumstances surrounding the main angle of the article.

The rest of the article will probably be written in chronological order, although it may be necessary to include other background information paragraphs as you go through.

Speech

Rather than using all reported speech, try to include snatches of conversation as direct speech as this will add authenticity and dynamism to your writing.

Closing paragraphs

Readers often assess whether to read an article or not based on the closing paragraph as well as the opening one. It makes for a more satisfying article if the end properly rounds off the piece rather than the story just petering out.

There are various types of endings:

- going back to the beginning
- surprise
- advice
- quotation
- anecdote
- looking forwards.

Transitions

While it is perfectly possible to write paragraphs in isolation from one another, it makes for more comfortable reading if transitions or linking words are used to connect them together.

Example:

Full of racy comment and salacious gossip, my memoirs will reveal just what goes on when the curtain goes down. Having spent many years in show business, I'm privy to many secrets about household names. Secrets they would prefer remained untold.

However, first let me talk about myself, a subject of abiding interest to all who know me. I was born, if not literally in a trunk, then certainly not far from one, my mother being a porter at Kings Cross Station.

The use of the word 'However' indicates that the writer is switching emphasis – in this case from talking about other people to talking about himself. This second paragraph would still make sense without 'However', but its inclusion makes the story flow better. Note also that the second paragraph also gives some background information.

Re-writes

If you can, leave the article alone for at least a day or two so that you can re-read it objectively. The best way to judge how well you have written it is to read it out aloud – better still, get someone else to read it out to you.

This will soon show up sentences which are too long or badly written as well as repetitious words and purple prose (those flights of fancy which we all include initially and then delete). It will also show if you have assembled the information in a coherent order, have given enough information for the readers to understand any references you might make and whether you have used sufficient transitions to make the piece flow.

Ambiguity

It is easy to get so focussed on what you are trying to say that you overlook the fact that the sentence can also mean something else entirely. This can be due to:

- A lack of clarity in the English language: 'They are eating apples' can mean that some people are eating apples, or that the apples are eating apples, not cooking apples.
- Word order: 'He went downstairs to put the cat out in his pyjamas.' This sounds as if the cat is wearing the pyjamas.
- The pronoun 'it': 'He let it in again because it was wet.' Here the first 'it' obviously refers to the cat but the second 'it' could be referring to the cat or the weather.

Again, reading your piece aloud may show up any ambiguities.

Titles and illustrations

Choosing a title

While you may already have a working title for your piece, which has helped you focus on what you planned to write, now is the time to select one which grabs the reader's attention, captures the spirit of what you have written and is appropriate for your chosen magazine.

It is quite likely that if your article is published it will appear under a different one because choosing titles is part of the sub editor's job as they will know what will fit in best. But that doesn't mean you don't have to bother because your title is the first thing the editor is going to look at. If it is bland and boring they may think it reflects the rest of the article and not read any further.

There are a number of different types of title including:

- questions: 'Why does it always happen to me?'
- quotations or sayings: 'All the world's a stage'
- puns: 'Many hands get in the way'
- alliteration: 'Teenage Tantrums'.

Illustrations

Most articles benefit from illustrations and some editors won't take them unless you can send photos as well. If you don't have any suitable ones it may be worth your while taking some specially for the article.

Make sure you own the copyright to any illustrations you send in.

Submission

When submitting your article firstly decide on your magazine, then telephone them and find out the following:

- Find out the name of the editor or the person you should send your article to. The quickest way to get your article binned is to address your letter 'Dear Sir or Madam'.
- Does the editor want a fully-written article or a proposal? Generally speaking editors prefer writers to send a proposal for an article first rather than the complete article, which they may not have time to read. So even though you may have written your article be prepared to send a proposal first if required.

- Is the editor happy to accept articles or proposals by email or do they prefer post? Many magazines now prefer emailed articles because it saves someone inputting them on the computer.

> **Top tip**
> Double check how to spell the editor's name.

For guidelines on how to submit articles see Appendix A.

How it's done

Someone who has successfully written articles about her life is Edna Lydiate.

> **Case study**
>
> I retired at the age of 60 in 2002 and thought I would like to do a creative writing course at Runshaw College in Leyland. I had studied all the social sciences since 1995 and written many essays, but never dared attempt creative writing. I thought the others in the class would be successful writers and I would feel out of my depth.
>
> A friend suggested that I practise my skills on *Yours* magazine as they were always looking for life articles and my son suggested *Chat* magazine. So I wrote to both. To my surprise I received £50 from *Chat* for my spooky story about a premonition I had at work that a window was going to fall in. I told the girls not to sit under it and they all laughed. Two weeks later the window fell in.
>
> *Yours* magazine then accepted my story 'Look for a Silver Lining When Things go Wrong'. It made a full page in the magazine, but there was no payment. This gave me the confidence to go to Runshaw College to do the creative writing course and I was amazed to find that I was the only one in the class who had ever had anything published.
>
> Since then I have written many short stories about my life and together there is now enough to turn into a book using my own photographs to illustrate it. They include 'The House Where I was Born', 'My Childhood Memories', 'My Teenage Years', 'Brother and Sister', and 'A Grand Day Out Riding my Scooter in 1960', which made a two-page spread in *Yours* magazine that paid £75.
>
> I don't get bored writing articles about me and would recommend it to anyone as a way of starting writing their life story.
>
> Edna Lydiate

Analyzing an article

'A Grand Day Out Riding my Scooter in 1960' became 'A Mod and Her Scooter' in *Yours* magazine and the full article is printed below with my analysis of it.

> *I was 18 in 1960 and I remember those youthful years as a golden time – I never looked back and I never sat still. I had what seemed like millions of friends – and I had more energy packed into my five foot one and a half-inch frame than the lot of them!*

This opening paragraph fulfils all the rules. In two sentences, and using only 52 words, Edna sets the scene for a nostalgic look back, as well as intriguing the reader. Not one word is wasted, there is no waffle and she has used the active form of the verbs. For information about the active and passive form of verbs see Chapter 13.

> *You could say I was a Mod. I had a brand-new BSA Sunbeam 175cc scooter. Not being very tall, when my scooter was stationary, just my toes touched the road, so I always had to make sure I stopped near a pavement to keep my balance.*

This is the nub paragraph which connects the opening paragraph with the rest of the article and indicates that it is going to be about Edna's adventures on her scooter.

> *I was a member of Preston Scooter Club and we went out on our scooters every Sunday – to the Lake District or Yorkshire – somewhere different every week. A gallon of petrol (around 32p) would take you anywhere for the day.*

> *The scooter club rented a room over the top of Carter's Pram Shop in Ribbleton Lane where we'd meet on a Thursday night to play darts, table tennis and records, and arrange the next Sunday ride. Even in winter we rode out. We froze, but it was worth it – we loved our scooters.*

These two paragraphs add some background information to scooter owning. The inclusion of the cost of petrol at that time adds some historic detail and the final sentence '*We froze, but it was worth it – we loved our scooters*', adds emotional detail. This was a love affair.

> *In the true spirit of women's lib, wearing overalls, I changed the oil and serviced the scooter myself. I did this at night in the garage where I worked in the office as a bookkeeper/typist during the day.*

This paragraph tells us a bit more about Edna herself. Again she has used the active form of the verbs to give her writing some dynamism.

In the passive form it would have been written: 'In the true spirit of women's lib and wearing overalls, the oil was changed and the scooter was serviced by me. It was done at night in the garage where I worked as a bookkeeper/typist during the day.' This is a much stodgier way of writing.

> One Sunday ride was to the Yorkshire Dales. I'd just had a windscreen fitted on my scooter, but it was very windy, and we were doing 40 mph (very speedy!). On the way to Kirby Lonsdale the wind blew me across the road, up on to the banking and I came to a halt in the middle of a field – it was like riding a bucking bronco!
>
> As I was riding at the tail end of 12 scooters I wasn't missed until the group came to a road junction. They backtracked to look for me and saw me pushing my scooter down the bank. After that they kept the speed down to 30 mph and suggested I took a pillion passenger with me on the next ride – or get rid of the windscreen!
>
> So Valerie hopped on the back with me and she also came with me on my first scooter holiday, to Rhyl for a week in 1961. We stayed at a guest house which was full of teenagers from Manchester. We made friends and had some lovely days out with them. The landlady banned us from visiting each other's rooms. She said 'it wasn't proper'. So much for the liberated sixties!

Edna uses transition words at the start of the last two paragraphs: 'As' and 'So'. These words join the paragraphs together to show that they are all connected. They could be left out, but the three paragraphs would not flow so well.

The sentence 'It was like riding a bucking bronco' is a good use of description.

> We had a mishap the day we went to Caernarvon. I turned off the main street into a little side street that led up a very steep hill which was too much for my scooter to climb with two of us riding it. The scooter stalled halfway up. 'Quick, Valerie, jump off!' I shouted as the scooter started sliding backwards on the wet cobbled street towards the terraced houses at the bottom...

I reversed right into some poor unsuspecting woman's open front door, coming to a halt with the back wheel inside the porch and the front wheel on the doorstep. The lady was livid, shouting at me in Welsh, her arms flying about.

A grinning passer-by said, 'She is calling you a lunatic and is going to send for the police.' With that, I swiftly pushed the scooter back on to the road and shouted to Valerie, 'Jump on quick, and let's get out of here.' She climbed on, I kick-started the engine and we never stopped until we found a cafe outside the town, where we began to see the funny side of it.

The use of direct speech in the above paragraphs adds greatly to the dynamism and urgency of the situation. Reported speech would have slowed the action down. There is also a good use of adjectives: *'wet cobbled streets', 'a grinning passerby'.*

The following year I drove my scooter to the Isle of Wight with another friend and stayed at a guest house in Sandown. The ferry boat jerked while setting sail and my scooter fell over, smashing another windscreen.

The main body of the article has been written in chronological order and it all flows.

Reluctantly, after three years riding my scooter, I gave it up while I was still in one piece. In that time, I broke three windscreens, fell off twice, and was knocked off by a car and nearly killed.

If this was a chapter in a life story, the writer would undoubtedly have gone into details about how she was nearly killed, but as this is a light-hearted article Edna is right to merely mention it.

But there was nothing to compare with the feeling when I set off on the scooter with the engine purring beneath me, in complete control of its every movement (well, most of the time!).

This is an excellent closing paragraph. It sums up how Edna felt about her scooter-riding days and ends with an ironic note.

The whole article has been written in a humorous vein and with a light touch. She has varied the length of her sentences and has also made good use of dashes and brackets to emphasize certain points, as well as a reasonable sprinkling of exclamation marks.

Exercise

Select an incident from your life and turn it into either a letter or an article.

Spend time choosing and writing the opening paragraph and choosing the title.

Send it to a magazine.

Summary

In this chapter you have learnt:

- how to write an opening paragraph
- how use transitions
- how to choose a title
- how to analyze an article.

07

preparing to write

In this chapter you will learn:
- how to get started
- how to overcome writer's block
- how to set writing targets.

A man may write at any time, if he will set himself doggedly to it.

Samuel Johnson

If getting material together is a bit like gardening, then getting ready to write can be a bit like preparing for a race.

Firstly, don't let the enormity of the task put you off. Remember, every marathon run and every mountain climbed is done by putting one foot after the other – no more than that. Writing is just the same, you just put down one word after the other. It needs some stamina and commitment, but unless you have a publisher setting you a deadline, you can work at your own pace. If you want to write it in a week, that's fine. If you want to take years, that's fine too.

The next point to remember is that to start with you are only writing a first draft. All that matters is that you get something down on paper: don't worry about grammar, spelling or style as these can all be sorted out in the second draft.

Finally, make sure you are physically comfortable with writing. If you prefer to write in longhand with a notepad and pencil – as my mother did – then that is the right way for you to do it. If you try to force yourself to use something different you may give up: not because you don't want to write the book, but because you are struggling with technology.

Depending on what you want to do with your life story you can always get it typed up or put on a computer. There are plenty of professional typists who can do this for you, but they will obviously charge for this.

If you are able to use a computer then this is the best option. It is easier to correct errors and make alterations. It also has a spellchecker, although you can't rely on this entirely.

As you may be writing for comparatively long periods you need to be sitting comfortably. If you are using a laptop it might be better to have it on a table at the right height rather than balanced on the arm of a chair or on your lap.

It also helps to have sufficient space to be able to spread your material out, and to be able to leave it out, rather than packing everything away each day.

Many writers have rituals they have to go through before they start writing such as lining up their pencils or making a cup of coffee. This is fine, but don't let these turn into an excuse not to write. If you start finding tasks which need to be done before you can begin to work, such as doing the ironing, mowing the lawn or cleaning the car, then you may have to consider whether you really want to do this.

> **Top tip**
> If using a computer get into the habit of regularly saving as you write by clicking on the floppy disk icon otherwise an unexpected power failure or surge could wipe out what you have just written.

Getting started

As this is a first draft you can start it anyway you want to. When you sit down to write a letter it is unlikely that you worry about starting it. You know who you are writing to and you know what you are going to say. Treat your book in the same way: think of someone that you are describing your life story to and literally start it, Dear... You can delete their name when it is finished.

It isn't even necessary to start at the beginning. If you want to write about your time in Africa or getting married before writing the earlier chapters on where you were born that's fine.

If you are still struggling for words, it might just be a question of priming the pump, so write a description of something familiar such as the house where you were born, or what your father wore to work. The secret is to get something, anything, written so that your mind gets into the writing mode. Once you have got going then you can start writing your life story. What you have written to prime the pump may be used somewhere, but even if it isn't it has served its purpose and got you going.

How long will it take?

This is a bit like saying how long is a piece of string? Few people sit down at a computer and dash off 3,000 words before breakfast, but even if you only wrote 100 words a day, the same amount as on a large postcard, you would still be able to write a 60,000 word book in under two years.

Of course, not everyone is going to want to write a long life story. My mother's was around 12,000 words, which with family pictures makes a reasonable size book. She just wrote when she felt like it, perhaps once or twice a week. Sometimes she wrote between 10 and 20 pages on her notepad and other times she wrote less.

Writing your life story should be enjoyable so don't put yourself under so much pressure to finish it quickly that you make yourself miserable. On the other hand, if you are planning a full-length book, without some kind of timetable you might not finish it at all.

There are two ways of setting yourself regular goals:

- by time
- by words.

By time

To find time to write your life story you may have to make adjustments to your timetable so that you can fit in a regular period every day or every week for writing. How long this period is will depend on your circumstances. However, if it is too short, you will have just got going when it is time to stop. On the other hand don't feel you have to spend hours every day, that would be tiring and perhaps counter-productive.

If time is not a problem then spending two or three hours a day will soon see the book written. But even those with busy lives will find with a bit of adaptability they can spend more time writing than they may have first realized.

Writing for two hours a day doesn't all have to be done in one go. An hour or so can be stolen by getting up earlier or going to bed later – depending on whether you are an early bird or a night owl – or by watching less television. Another half an hour can be added at lunchtime. If you know you want to write then it is amazing how much more quickly you can get through tasks such as ironing, cutting the grass or washing up to give you another 30 minutes.

If you only have a short amount of time each day then it is essential to use that time constructively. Making a chart where you can plot what you want to achieve each day can act as an incentive.

> **Top tip**
> Try to finish one day's work with a note on how to start the next day's so that you don't waste time wondering what to write.

By words

If you don't like to be tied to the clock then giving yourself a regular quota of words to write might be a better option. Some people can write several thousand words a day, others will struggle to complete a few hundred. It doesn't matter how many you decide to write at a time, what is important is that you complete that quota before the end of the day. You can write them all in one sitting or, as above, write a portion of them when you can during the day.

Whichever way you decide to write, the way to complete the book is to get into a regular habit because writing, like all forms of activity, needs to be practised on a regular basis – the more you do it the easier it becomes.

Top tip

Remember to set realistic targets. If you are over ambitious and then start to fall behind you may become demoralized and give up.

Waiting for the muse

Is it better to write only when the mood takes you or should you try to get something written even if what you write is rubbish?

This will depend on your circumstances. If you have plenty of time, then perhaps it is better to go out and play a round of golf or visit a friend rather than fume over a hot computer.

However, professional writers can't wait for the muse to strike, they just get on with it. As I said above, the more regularly you write the easier it will become.

Remember it is not essential to write your story starting at the beginning and working your way through to the end. So if you are stuck on one chapter move on to the next. You can come back to the unfinished one at a later date.

Top tip

Don't forget to back your work up on to a CD, flash drive or external hard drive when you have finished for the day.

Writer's block

Although in theory you shouldn't have writer's block because you know exactly what you are writing and who you are writing about, it can still happen that you find yourself staring at a blank piece of paper or computer screen, and can't think of a word to say.

This may be because you haven't collected enough information or done enough research. So stop writing and start researching.

Alternatively, you may have too much background information and be struggling to cope with it all. In this case you may need to be ruthless and prune it. You can always add more information during the second draft if it is necessary.

Perhaps you have set yourself too high a target. Lower the number of words you want to write every day down to 50 – even less if you are still struggling, or cut your writing time down to ten minutes. When your new target has been achieved stop work. Over the next few days gradually increase the target back to where it was.

Maybe you need to re-motivate yourself and there are various ways of doing this:

- Read some more memoirs, particularly those which are similar to what you are planning to write.
- Watch a film from the era you're writing about, or read a book, or look through old newspapers and magazines.
- Look for a writers' group. Writing in the main is a solitary occupation and with the best will in the world your family may not understand what you are struggling with. If you can find a good group then discussing your problems with like-minded people will at least ensure you get a sympathetic hearing and probably lots of practical help as well. (See Appendices for information on finding a group.)
- Start a writers' group if you can't find one. You may be surprised at how many people there are out there writing memoirs, novels etc. and who all want to get in touch with other writers. See if you can get your local paper interested in doing a story about your trying to start a group.
- Try networking with other writers through chat rooms or blogging sites.

Keeping going

There comes a point in all writing, particularly with a project that is going to take weeks rather than days, when it is a struggle to keep going: in other words, you have hit the writers' equivalent of the doldrums.

This usually happens about halfway through, when the first flush of enthusiasm has worn off. You wonder if what you are doing is worthwhile or whether anyone is going to be interested in reading your life story – or even whether you will have the stamina to finish it. This is normal: most of us suffer from self doubt when we are writing and there are certainly times when we wonder if we will ever get to the end.

So because it is so normal there is no need to worry about it – just dig deep, grit your teeth and keep going. If it helps, keep checking the number of words you have written just to prove that you are adding to your total, however slowly.

> **Top tip**
> If you are writing your story for your grandchildren, keep their picture on your desk to put pressure on yourself to finish it.

The good news is that once you are past this section you can usually get to the end quite easily and you will suddenly find you have completed your first draft.

Rewards

These are important and you deserve them. When you have finished the day's allocated work – and not before – give yourself a cup of tea, a glass of whisky or whatever is your favourite treat. If you are writing on a computer, check your word count to see how much you have written.

When you have finished a chapter have a day or two off from writing. Do something completely different with your time: this will re-energize you. Add up the word counts for each chapter and when you have reached 5,000 give yourself another treat. And do the same for 10,000 and 20,000 and so on.

Don't worry if you think that by having a day or two off from writing you will lose the thread or write in a different style. That can all be resolved when you come to the second draft.

When you have completely finished the first draft then it is essential to walk away from it for at least a week if not more. If you can, take a holiday to put it right out of your mind. This is not only a just reward for all your hard work, but it is also necessary. You need to come back to the book in a totally objective frame of mind because your next task is to be ruthless about what else has to be put in – and what has to come out.

Exercise

Set your targets.

Plan your rewards.

Summary

In this chapter you have learnt:

- how to set writing goals
- how to re-motivate yourself
- the importance of rewards.

08

organizing your material

In this chapter you will learn:
- different ways to structure your book
- how to divide it into chapters
- how to handle your information.

The two offices of memory are collection and distribution.

Samuel Johnson

Once you have written your notes and collected lots of other information and background detail it's time to work out how you are going to pull it all together to create a manuscript. I shall call it a manuscript for now because turning it into a book comes later.

If you have already written part of it in the form of articles or letters you are well on your way. It will then just be a question of fitting the other information around them.

While you have been collecting memories and information you will probably have decided what type or genre of life story you want to write – if you haven't, then look again at the options in Chapter 01. You may also find it helpful to read different types of life stories, memoirs and autobiographies to help you decide.

Top tip

Don't forget to read those by 'ordinary' writers as well as those by well-known writers because the former may be more helpful to you.

Having decided on the type or genre, then you will need to decide when your life story is going to start and finish. Unless it is going to be your whole life, it is a good idea to start and finish on specific dates, for specific reasons, such as from birth to leaving school, or your wedding day to your diamond wedding day. These then act like bookends to your story and hold it together. Otherwise there is a danger that your book might just peter out because you don't know how to end it.

But don't forget, these decisions are not set in stone, in the course of writing you might decide to expand the time frame or reduce it – or even change it altogether.

Once you have a good idea of what kind of book you are aiming for the next decisions to make are:

- What will be its structure?
- How will it be divided into chapters?
- What information will go in each chapter?

Structure

There are several different ways of structuring a life story:

- chronological order
- flashbacks
- diary form
- vignettes or cameos
- anecdotes
- themes and topics
- fictionalized (this is dealt with in Chapters 14 and 15).

Chronological order

This is probably the most usual structure especially if you are writing for family and friends. It is also the simplest: you start from the date you decide to begin your life story with and work your way through.

However, this doesn't mean there won't be an element of flashbacks: it is sometimes necessary to explain something which has happened in the past to make sense of what you are writing about.

Sometimes it may be necessary to flash forward as well because even though your story might end at a certain period your readers will want to know what happened to 'so-and-so' a few years down the line.

Of course there will always be some information which can't be neatly slotted in and may warrant a chapter on its own.

> **Top tip**
> Even if you write the first draft in chronological order there is nothing to stop you changing the order in the final manuscript.

Flashbacks

While it is likely that most life stories have an element of flashbacks within them, there is a specific format where the writer reveals the whole of their life story through a series of flashbacks.

A common way is to start the story in the present and fill in the past details through a series of flashbacks. Sometimes the flashbacks are in chronological order, but this isn't strictly necessary provided the reader is always made aware of which point in time is being written about.

Example:

Opera singer Lesley Garrett's life story *Notes from a Small Soprano* starts with a prologue in the present briefly describing her last 12 months and the decision that now was the time to write her life story.

Some books have a more complicated structure where the writer starts from a particular point and moves forward chronologically and at the same time inter-cuts their story with flashbacks to earlier times.

Examples:

Blake Morrison, in his life story *And when did you last see your Father?* uses this technique. Chapters describing his father's last days are inter-cut with chapters of his memories of his childhood and growing up. Ricky Tomlinson uses the same technique in his autobiography *Ricky*.

Diary form

What makes diaries fascinating is that they contain accounts of people and events which are contemporaneous rather than memories which have been filtered through time. For this reason the fewer alterations you make to them the better. Resist the temptation to tidy them up or make changes because of hindsight.

However, you may want to add some footnotes if you need to explain an entry or to add background information – and it is a good idea to leave out the boring bits and concentrate on those days which had the most drama in them.

You may also have to make a decision on whether to include the highly personal or explicit entries.

Example:

The late Alan Clark MP, who published three volumes of his diaries, said that he 'excised' a lot of entries, but what remained he didn't alter.

Vignettes or cameos

In this format you choose to write about the most interesting, dramatic or life-changing incidents, which can often be separated by long periods of time. This technique ensures that only the really interesting parts of your life are included, while leaving out the more boring parts in between.

However, unless you are going to include short, linking chapters to fill in what happened in between those moments, it will sometimes be necessary to include this information within the vignette.

Example:

In Goldie Hawn's *A Lotus Grows in the Mud*, she gives vivid accounts of different times of her life and career while keeping her private life to herself.

Anecdotes

While anecdotes will often be included in all the other formats, it is possible to write a life story made up from nothing but anecdotes.

Example:

Arthur's Village is a series of anecdotes covering all aspects of rural life as seen through the young Arthur's eyes.

Hurdy gurdys, barrel organs and organ grinders

There were frequently travellers on the road with a barrel organ or a hurdy gurdy stopping to play outside the houses and then calling at doors in the hope of a copper or two for reward. I remember a decrepit old man calling occasionally, he had a box shaped instrument slung on his back which had one leg attached on which he rested it to play by turning the handle.

Teeth

About the year 1912 we were notified that a school dentist would be visiting the school and we also had a talk on dental care. For further encouragement we were offered toothbrushes which had to be ordered through the schoolmaster. They cost twopence each and I remember they were made of cane. Toothpowder of course, we were quite unacquainted with and we were told to use ordinary table salt as a cleaning agent.

Themes and topics

This could be a solution to those who find it difficult to write about themselves or to have themselves as the main subject. The theme or topic becomes the focus of the book and the writer's life story is revealed in relation to it.

The topics could range from pets owned to houses lived in or from friends and family to recipes collected.

Examples:

Nigel Slater's autobiography, *Toast*, is based on the theme of food and written under headings such as Christmas Cake, Bread and Butter Pudding and Sherry Trifle. Starting with his mother's haphazard cooking he tracks his childhood and adolescence through her illness and death, his stepmother's arrival on the scene, and his own early work in the catering industry.

Mary Lucas's book, *Lunchmeat and Life Lessons*, is written around the nuggets of wisdom given to her by her father. Her career in business as well as her family background is interwoven into the story.

This is also the structure chosen by Geoff Walford, who was forced to take three months' rest after a hip replacement.

Case study

All this for an active person like me was a bit of a shock. What could I usefully do to keep me occupied?

Then I thought, how about music? I was a trained singer having passed exams for the London College of Music, had spent many happy hours whilst living in Ormskirk (1963–84) performing in Lancashire and Yorkshire, with choirs and as a soloist, entering and winning prizes at music festivals etc. etc. In fact spending too much time singing as my wife reminded me constantly.

So why not put pen to paper under the heading: *A Life of Music 1963 to 1984 – up North*. I had all the material somewhere in the house it just needed putting together in some form of sequence. I had London College of Music results, festival certificates, concert programmes, press cuttings etc. from over the years. When I came to sit down and write there was a sequence of my music making and development.

I began with my early years as a choirboy in Brighouse, Yorkshire, complete with angelic photograph.

The 1960s were spent training, taking London College of Music examinations and starting life with the Ormskirk Orchestral and Musical Society both singing and being chairman at various times. Plenty of programmes and press cuttings (though a bit faded with time). Solo singing competitions at Huddersfield, Lytham St. Annes, Leyland, Wigan, winning quite a few in the tenor classes.

The 1970s saw me singing with the Ionian Singers a semi-professional group performing in the north west. I began solo singing of Oratorio works, Messiah, Elijah, etc. with various societies and so much enjoyed this period. In 1973 I began training with Barbara Dix (ex Glyndbourne Opera) and her husband Alex Abercrombie (concert pianist). It was the start of an exhilarating period of opera singing under Barbara's tutelage. I was encouraged to enter more competitions and had successes at Southport, Crosby, Blackpool, and Liverpool festivals.

I did have an audition to sing with the BBC Northern Singers and although I did well it would have meant a lot of time spent rehearsing and travelling which I could ill afford.

Opera then came much to the fore starring with the Mastersingers group which Barbara had formed. We did many operas – *Magic Flute, Carmen, Hansel and Gretel, Cinderella, La Boheme, Marriage of Figaro* at various venues, both concert and full costume performances.

It all sadly had to end when we moved south to Yatton in 1985 to be near our family.

But it's been a joy to record it all, so glad I did it (thanks to the hip replacement). I wrote it all in longhand, preserved in a lever arch file.

What next? Well I've made a start under the heading of: *You're in the Army now – Mate!* about my two years national service experience. Got some useful background papers but do need to research further with Google™ help.

Geoff Walford

Dividing it into chapters

If you are writing a straightforward life story then it will probably fall naturally into divisions such as:

- early childhood
- school days
- employment
- marriage
- family
- retirement.

But it could also be divided it into periods of time such as decades, years or months or into topics (see earlier).

Depending on how much information you have these chapters could be divided again, for example your early childhood could be divided into chapters on:

- where you were born
- what your house looked like
- what the city, town or village was like
- what your parents were like
- what your siblings were like.

Information which can't be slotted in under obvious headings, or which comes into more than one chapter, such as sporting interests or background information about your village, may need a chapter of its own.

Top tip

It is useful to name the chapters as this helps to clarify what goes in them, but these names may well get changed in the final draft where you will have scope to be much more imaginative.

Once you start writing you may find that some chapters need to be divided up and others amalgamated. Writing your life story is always going to be a fluid process and while you need to have an overall view of what you are trying to achieve it is also necessary to be adaptable. If your writing takes you off in a new and better direction, or you decide to delete one part and add something else, then that is the right thing to do.

Also some chapters are going to be longer than others either because you have remembered more about that particular period or because it was more important to you. But at this stage don't worry that your book will be unbalanced, the main thing is to get the first draft written.

Number of chapters

Again this will depend on how much information you have and how long you plan to make your book. If you are aiming for a book the size of this one, which is around 70,000 words, then you should probably aim for around 20 chapters. This will give you an average of 3,500 words per chapter – approximately the length of this chapter.

Headings

Once you have decided on your chapters then it is helpful to subdivide each one under a heading. For example, if you have a chapter describing your brothers and sisters you could give each one their own heading. This makes it easier to see where each piece of your information should go.

Whether you leave these headings in your final manuscript is a matter of personal preference.

No chapters

Of course you don't have to divide your book into chapters at all. If you life story is based on a series of anecdotes it can be written as one continuous chapter broken up with headings. This is the method used in *Arthur's Village* (see example of 'Anecdotes' earlier).

Handling your information

Depending on how extensive your research has been, you may have a considerable amount of information to feed into your life story, including all your notes, some family history, background detail and historical information.

This is where you will reap the benefit of writing your memories on separate cards or pieces of paper because your first task is to divide them up among your chapters and then further divide them among your headings. Then, using your timeline for reference, fill in the relevant dates under each heading to act as markers. These can be left in or taken out of the final draft.

> **Top tip**
> It also helps to make notes of what you intend to include under each heading so that you don't forget anything.

Now you have the skeleton of each chapter all you need to do is flesh it out with your memories, background information and any other details you want to include.

If you are undecided about what should be included and what should be left out try to think what you, as a reader, would want to see in a life story. For example, what is it that you would want to know about your grandparents had they written a book?

> **Top tip**
> Don't try to include everything in the first draft, just get the skeleton down on paper or the computer first.

The truth the whole truth and nothing but the truth

While you are spending time thinking about how to turn your life into chapters and headings this is probably the right time to take a good look at what you are proposing to write and how it will affect other people.

The truth

Truth is variously defined as being: genuine, factual, verified, the opposite of false. However, we all know that one person's remembrance of an event may be quite different from another's. We also know that our minds can play tricks and our memories are not always accurate. In fact sometimes it is not always easy to distinguish between what we actually remember for ourselves and what we have been told about a person or an event.

The more research you do, the more you cross-check your remembrances of events with those of family and friends, the more likely you are to write a truthful account. The main thing is that your readers should recognize the truth of what you're writing and not be thinking 'that's not how we remember it.'

Speech

It is perfectly acceptable to write down roughly what you or other people said at the time as it is unlikely that you will be able to recall the words exactly. However, it is unacceptable to put words into people's mouths that they couldn't possibly have said.

Even though you can't remember the exact words, try to use the normal speech patterns of the people concerned and include any words or phrases they regularly used.

The whole truth

Does your life story have to be a total, warts and all, account? No, it is up to you what you decide to put in and what you decide to leave out. While it will make your story more interesting if you include the bad times as well as the good – because these have all helped to shape you – you have the final control over what you want to include.

We all have some boring parts in our lives so it is a good idea to cut those out. And you are not compelled to put in any parts which are embarrassing or painful to you. Although, if you are writing for cathartic or therapeutic reasons then it probably will be necessary to include details of the traumas you have suffered.

By the same token, you should also take into account other people's feelings. It is all very well being honest about yourself, but do you have the right to be honest on behalf of other people? You may want to write about former partners or lovers, but will this hurt your current partner? Should you reveal that skeleton in the cupboard or should you let sleeping dogs lie? Look at what you plan to write and decide if anyone else will be hurt or embarrassed by your revelations, and whether it is better to be truthful or tactful.

Do you have all the facts? If your version of events is incorrect and other people's reputations suffer as a result you could find yourself sued for libel. Even if your version of events is correct, the people about whom you are writing could still have a case if you have shown them in an unflattering light. Changing names and details may not always be enough to protect their identity.

So if you are planning to include information which could be hurtful or surprising to someone else it might be a good idea to forewarn them, if only to stop a rift between family and friends. If they say they are happy for you to include it, it might also be a good idea to get that in writing.

Nothing but the truth

In other words should you embellish your story or make your life more exciting than it actually was? We all want to be the hero of our own story but how far should we go in putting ourselves forward and denying other people's contributions to events and situations?

No one expects you to be completely self-effacing – in fact a writer who constantly oozes false modesty can be very irritating. Equally readers soon notice when a writer enhances their role in events, so take care if you do decide to embellish the facts because you can be sure that someone will notice.

However, a bit of poetic licence is acceptable when describing events or telling an anecdote if this make them more humorous.

Shades of truth

How far you move away from the truth will depend on whether you are writing a strictly factual life story, a fictionalized version of it or a novel based on it (see Chapters 14 and 15). However, beware of claiming your book to be completely true if it isn't. Those who do this generally get found out.

Work in progress

My mother decided to restrict her life story to the period between 1916, when she was born, and 1948, when we moved into our first real home because she felt that this period would be of most interest to her grandchildren and great grandchildren – particularly as it covered a way of life, which has now disappeared.

Although she mentioned her sisters in the chapters on her early childhood and school years it was soon clear that they warranted a chapter of their own.

Example:

> *Doris was the only one of us to have the perfect traditional wedding. She met Jim Parsons, a local football hero and captain of Caterham Old Boys Football Club, at a dance. He was her first and only boyfriend and she was his first and only girlfriend.*

> *They married on my eighteenth birthday and Mabel and I were bridesmaids along with our cousin Olive. We all made our own dresses, which were long and made of flame-coloured satin. We wore those dresses long afterwards to many dances.*

> *Mabel's wedding was a complete contrast. She met Sidney Jeffes at the Mountain Pools. His father was a Consul at the British Embassy in Brussels. They had a Register Office wedding in Purley and no one was invited except Mum and Dad who went as witnesses. After the service Mum and Dad came straight home and Mabel and Sidney drove off for their honeymoon in Cornwall – Sidney changing out of his suit in the car.*

From *Another Girl* by Florence Herbert

Exercise

Break your story down into chapters.

Put headings in your first chapter.

Select the notes, background information and other data to go under each of these headings.

Summary

In this chapter you have learnt:

- how to handle your information
- how to structure your book
- how truthful your story should be.

09

first draft

In this chapter you will learn:
- how to analyze structure
- how to find your style
- how to use direct speech.

Writing when properly managed, (as you may be sure I think mine is) is but a different name for conversation.

Laurence Sterne

Now that you have your chapters, headings and notes it is time to get something down on paper or the computer. Some people get very worried about this stage but remember, it is your life story and you can tell it however you choose. No one will be giving you marks out of ten, or covering it with red biro! In other words there is no right or wrong way of doing this; all that matters is that you start writing.

Keep it simple, keep it natural and don't let any worries about not being any good at grammar or spelling put you off. This is only a first draft and any errors can be sorted out once you have finished it.

If it still seems a bit daunting, take a look at how other writers do it.

Reading other life stories

It doesn't matter whether these are books you have already read or whether they are new to you, because this time you will be less interested in the story being told and more interested in the type of life story, its construction and the voice of the writer.

To some extent it also doesn't matter if they are badly written because you can learn almost as much from these as from well-written ones – even if it is only what to avoid.

Construction

It is not always easy to put our finger on why some life stories are much easier to read than others but analyzing the following may provide some clues:

- Style: If the writer is someone you know have they written in the same way as they talk or have they used a different style? Does the style fit their story or does it feel false?
- Tone: Is it formal, informal or chatty?
- Speech: Have they used direct speech as well as reported speech?
- Accents and dialects: How have they written words in a different accent or dialect? Has it been done well or is it irritating?

Finding your style

Use what you have read to help you, but don't let it influence your writing to the extent that you are copying them. This is your story and it needs to be told your way. So here are some tips on how to find your own style.

Voice

Each of us has a voice, a particular way that we speak. It is the product of where we were born and brought up, our family background, our education and our peer groups. It comes from the type of words we use – such as archaic, pedantic, slangy or colloquial – and the way we put these words together, such as sentence length and construction.

To see how different writers have different voices look again at Edna Lydiate's article in Chapter 06 and then compare it with the two examples below – both are telling anecdotes, but in quite different voices.

Examples:

The rainwater was also used for our bath night – usually Fridays, when we had our weekly bath in the kitchen for which mother kept an extra large zinc bath tub – and what a performance that was! Here again the water had to be dipped out or carried out, and during the baths the temperature had to be maintained by adding a kettle of boiling water occasionally. If the kettle took a long time to boil the last one or two had to endure the misery of tepid water.

From *Arthur's Village* by Arthur Westcott

I shared a tiny cabin with three other ladies, all strangers to me, as was the way when booking cruises on the cheap, and spent most of my time falling over everyone's luggage. However, since their interests were substantially different from my own our paths rarely crossed and we really only met at dressing time before dinner. Cheaper cabins didn't in those days sport ensuite facilities, so showers were communal and dotted round the ship, perhaps two per corridor. This meant a hopeful dash with towels and shampoo, and the ladies toilets were places where we all beautified ourselves before appearing in the restaurant in our posh frocks.

From *Song of the Spinning Sun* by Mary Frances

We don't normally give our voice a thought when we are speaking and we probably don't worry about it when writing letters – but when it comes to writing something like a life story there is a temptation to change our voice in the belief that this is somehow different.

To guard against this and to ensure that your voice is recognizably you – **write as you speak** – but without the hesitations, repetitions and unfinished sentences. Your readers are reading your life story not someone else's and they want to hear your authentic voice.

Of course this is easier said than done when you first start writing, so try a little test to find your voice. Think of an incident from your life and write a brief description of it for:

- a solicitor
- a business colleague
- a close family member or friend.

Examples:

To a solicitor – When I was about three years old I had a frightening experience. I remember I went with my grandfather to feed the bakery's horses. While my grandfather put the hay in the horse's hayracks, I decided to get the oats out of the feed bins. These were made of galvanized metal and very deep. I could see the oats were a long way down. As I reached over I fell in head first. I was rescued by my grandfather who pulled me out by my feet.

To a business colleague – One of my first memories involving horses was when I was about three. As usual I had tagged along behind Grandad when he went across the road to feed the bakery's horses. I knew the oats were kept in deep galvanized metal bins in the feed room so while Grandad was throwing hay into the horses' hayracks I thought I'd get the oats for him. Unfortunately the bin was nearly empty and the oats were a long way down. As I leaned over gravity took its course and I went in head first and was stuck upside down. Grandad rescued me by grabbing my ankles and pulling me out. I was probably only stuck like that for a minute or so, but I can still remember the sheer terror of being trapped upside down in the dark.

To a friend – I'll never forget the time I tipped head first into an oat bin and got stuck upside down. I was about three and it's the first real horsey memory I have. I'd gone across the road with Grandad to help him feed the bakery's horses. Anyway, while he was chucking hay into the hayracks I thought I'd be helpful and get the oats. Problem was the bin, a deep galvanized thing, was nearly empty. I leant over further and further then whoosh, in I went. I'm not in there long before Grandad yanks me out by the ankles, but I tell you it was absolutely, ruddy terrifying, stuck there in the dark.

When you have written your three descriptions, choose the style you feel most comfortable with and which is suitable for your genre. Then write your life story as if you are having a conversation with that person and you are describing it to them.

It doesn't matter how wordy the first draft is, there will be plenty of time to tidy it up later.

Ask a friend

If you are concerned that you are adopting a special or unnatural writing style ask a good friend to check your manuscript to see if they recognize your voice. Don't let them start trying to re-write it though.

Watch your language

Beware of letting your language become formalized just because you are writing. For example, if you have always called your parents Mum and Dad don't start referring to them as Mother and Father. It's fine to be formal when you first introduce them, but after that write about them naturally.

The same applies to family nicknames or other special names. If you had nicknames for people or if they had nicknames for you, then use them. But don't forget to explain them to the reader, even if you are writing for a family which is familiar with them.

> **Top tip**
> You may find that you start by writing with a slightly formal voice but once you get going you adopt a more natural style. The earlier writing can then be re-written.

Expletives

Although the advice is 'write how you speak', you will need to decide whether this means including expletives and four-letter words. Undoubtedly there is a more relaxed attitude towards them these days, and if you are accustomed to sprinkling your conversation with a few it will look odd to leave them out. But the criterion has to be, who are you writing for and will they be offended? One alternative is to use dots or asterisks to fill in the missing words.

Direct speech

Many life stories are written entirely using reported speech, but it will help to bring your story alive if you also include some direct speech.

Examples:

With reported speech – When you are horse mad, you are prepared to ride any pony that's offered to you – with or without a saddle. While bareback riding puts you in close contact with the horse it is much harder to stop them if they decide to run off with you. And that is exactly what happened when Nobby, the greengrocer's pony, decided to head for home faster than I had intended. I could hear Wendy, who was waiting for her turn for a ride calling out for me to pull on the reins and to stop galloping off. I replied that I was trying, but when I pulled on them I shot up Nobby's neck.

With direct speech – When you are horse mad, you are prepared to ride any pony that's offered to you – with or without a saddle. While bareback riding puts you in close contact with the horse it is much harder to stop them if they decide to run off with you.

Even with the wind rushing past my ears I could hear Wendy shouting, 'Stop galloping about, it's my turn to ride him.'

'I can't stop him,' I shouted back, 'he's heading for home.'

'So pull on the reins,' she screamed, 'pull on the reins.'

'What do you think I'm trying to do,' I screamed back as I pulled on the reins and promptly shot up his neck.

Accents and dialect

Accents are to do with the way words are pronounced in different parts of the country such as 'Mum' and 'Mam'. Dialects are concerned with vocabulary, grammar and the way words are arranged in a sentence.

While you want to be as truthful as possible about how someone spoke, accents and dialects are usually difficult to write phonetically and even more difficult to read. Try to give a flavour of their speech by using the way they constructed their sentences and their favourite sayings.

Using some of their special vocabulary will also add flavour to your writing, although you may have to explain what it means to the reader.

Getting help

If you find you are struggling to get anything worthwhile written then it might be time to get some practical help rather than getting depressed.

Creative writing classes

Why not get some hands-on advice by joining a creative writing class. Most areas have them whether they are run by local colleges, Adult Education Centres, The Open University (OU) www.open.ac.uk, the University of the Third Age (U3A) www.u3a.org.uk/ or the Workers Educational Association (WEA) www.wea.org.uk/.

Many of these courses are listed in *The Writer's Handbook* or the *Writers' and Artists' Yearbook*. Colleges and Adult Education Centres are usually listed in the *Yellow Pages*. You can also track down courses through the Internet: put 'writing classes' into a search engine and follow the links.

As well as learning new writing skills you may also get feedback on your writing and help and encouragement from other members of the class.

Home courses

There are also numerous home courses available to help you learn how to write. Again you can find information on the Internet or in the magazines which specialize in helping people with their writing. With these you can work at your own rate and receive feedback from a tutor.

Residential courses

These offer the opportunity for concentrated learning in a literary environment. There are centres around the country as well as abroad. Courses can vary in length from a day to a week or more. Information can be found in *The Writer's Handbook*, the *Writers' and Artists' Yearbook* or the Internet.

Ghost writers

Finally, if you really feel you can't write your life story yourself then an alternative might be to use a ghost writer. If you can't find a member of your family or a friend to do it there are professional writers who will take on the task. This is not a cheap option, but if you don't have the time, or are struggling to find the words, at least it will ensure that your story is told.

It is obviously easier if you can find someone locally because they will probably want to meet with you to find out what kind of story you want written. It will also be necessary to give them the various notes you've made and documents you've collected that you want included.

Finding someone by word of mouth or personal recommendation is obviously the best option. Otherwise ask to see samples of their work, preferably something which has been published. Ensure that you have the final say in how it is written and that you own the copyright.

Work in progress

My mother found that initially she was adopting a formal style of writing, but once she got past the first two chapters she slipped naturally into her own style.

Exercise

Read a life story and analyze its structure.

Write an anecdote in a formal, informal and chatty form.

Write an anecdote using reported speech then re-write it using direct speech.

Summary

In this chapter you have learnt:

- how to find your voice
- when to use direct speech
- where to find help.

10

second draft

In this chapter you will learn:
- how to revise
- how to add emotional content
- how to add verbal colour.

Are you writing the truth?

Suppose someone has a different version? Opinions – and memories – vary.

Perhaps it would be wiser to omit this bit. Only you can decide...

Christine Franklin, tutor, Writers' News course,
'Making the most of your life experiences'

If writing the first draft is all about getting words down on paper then the second draft is all about turning those words into a readable life story.

Although some revising will be done while you are writing the first draft, it is better to do the main revision when you have got to the end of your manuscript.

The process is similar to that used in writing an article. The first requirement is to leave your manuscript alone for at least a week so that you can come back to it refreshed, and ready to be objective. Remember, the hard work has been done and this is the enjoyable part.

First read-through

This first read-through is to get an overall feel for book:

- Are some chapters too long?
- Are others too short?
- Are the chapters in the best order?
- Does it need extra chapters?
- Are one or more chapter superfluous?

Because this may be the first time that you have read the whole manuscript in one go it will also show if you have repeated the same information in two or more different chapters.

Top tip

It can be quite difficult, and tiring, to read an entire book on a computer screen and it is easy to miss errors so either enlarge the font size temporarily to make it easier, or print it off. If you print with double spacing you will have space to make notes about alterations and additions.

Chapters too long

Check to see if you have included unnecessary waffle or repetition. Readers will want to know all the small, everyday details, but there may be some parts which are a bit dull or repetitive and could be deleted.

Have you included information which might fit better in another chapter? If so move it there. Otherwise try to find a natural dividing place and cut them in two.

Chapters too short

Is there any other background information which could be included? Would it be beneficial to your life story to do a bit more research and add extra background detail? Otherwise see if any of the chapters can be amalgamated.

The best order

No matter how much trouble we take when deciding on the order of our chapters, when we come to read it through we may find that they don't flow properly or logically (I'm speaking from experience here). If you feel that this is happening to you, then move the chapters around until you find the best order.

For example, you might have put the chapter on your family tree right at the beginning because this seemed a logical place for it, but in fact a better place might be after chapters describing your grandparents.

The same applies to information within the chapter: is it in the right order or is it even in the right chapter? If it isn't then try moving it.

Extra chapters

Perhaps you realize that you have left out some important aspect of your life or have forgotten to mention people who meant a lot to you. Sometimes this information can be added to existing chapters, but if that isn't possible then slot in an extra chapter or two. The people you left out won't know that they were added as an afterthought unless you tell them.

The same applies if you feel that some more background information is needed to make sense of what happened or to clarify events. Even if you are writing for family and friends you also need to include information explaining who was related to whom, where everyone lived etc. because your book could be handed down to future generations or read by people unconnected with you – and they will appreciate these details.

Superfluous chapters

Conversely some chapters may appear unnecessary. Perhaps the relevant information in them can be fed into the other chapters or perhaps they could be deleted altogether.

Second read-through

This time you will be checking to see if you need to add:

- more detail
- anecdotes
- direct speech
- emotional content
- verbal colour
- senses
- characterization
- reflection
- voice.

More detail

While the first draft has been written in broad brush strokes now is the time to add the kind of details which will make your story come alive for the reader such as:

- what your engagement ring looked like
- what you wore when you went to your first dance.

Then there are the background details which add an extra dimension such as:

- interesting facts about the houses, villages, towns, countries you've lived in
- what the weather was like and how it affected what you were doing
- the local, national or world political situation and how it affected you and your family.

Readers will also want to know specific details such as:

- exact dates when events happened
- what make of car you were driving when you passed your test
- what number bus stopped outside your house.

Anecdotes

Now that you have the basis for your story drafted, are there any amusing, dramatic or perhaps harrowing stories which can be included.

Examples:

Harold and the Bees!

I can just remember too that in the garden beneath the kitchen window uncle had three or four hives of bees. They were in the old style straw skips on wooden stands. That was the time, I believe, when to take the honey the bees had to be destroyed over a sulphur pit. Brother Harold was curious enough to poke a stick into the entrance of one of the hives with the result that he was badly stung. I remember the commotion it caused and the 'blue-bag' was much in evidence.

From *Arthur's Village* by Arthur Westcott

Or Mary Lucas arriving back at her hotel after a sumptuous dinner out with company executives.

As I was getting ready for bed, I walked in to the bathroom thinking that these were indeed good and happy times. I looked in the mirror and smiled at myself. That is when I saw it. There it was, wedged right smack-dab in the centre of my two front teeth, a huge chunk of pepper staring back at me! It almost looked as if I had blacked out my two front teeth. I mean, it was huge!

I realized there is no way that it could have gone unnoticed by my executive companions.

At first, I just wanted to die right then and there, but then I just shook my head and laughed aloud, recalling my father's advice from the day before.

'You're right, Dad,' I thought to myself, as I brushed my teeth. 'Nobody can make you happy but yourself.'

Truth be told, in spite of that hunk of pepper, I was a very happy girl. I was seriously enjoying the ride I was on, and grateful to be on it.

From *Lunchmeat and Life Lessons* by Mary Lucas

Direct speech

If you haven't included any direct speech does your story need some? Places which might benefit are:

- the more dramatic moments: when it can heighten tension
- humorous moments
- when showing a person's particular use of certain words or phrases.

Have you got the right balance between direct and speech reported? Too much direct speech can be tiring to read, particularly if it isn't clear who is speaking.

Emotional content

As well as knowing what happened and why it happened, your readers will also want to know how you felt about it. This will make a connection between you and them, which will stretch down through generations.

Writing about your emotions covers both how you felt during happy times as well as sad ones. The former is usually easiest to write about such as your feelings on your wedding day, watching a beautiful sunset or taking that once-in-a-lifetime holiday.

The loss of a loved one, the break-up of a relationship or the descent into depression etc. are more difficult to write because as a nation we do tend to have stiff upper lips and don't like parading our emotions in public. The criterion to use when deciding what to include is: are you comfortable with what you have written and will you still be comfortable with it once it is in print?

Example:

My marriage disintegrated and my husband married someone else.

The following few years were probably the most difficult in my adult life. But although times were hard, I was not inclined to show the world how hard they were. One of the problems with emotional pain is that it is impossible to share without running in to pity (which can be unbearable) or the 'Pull yourself together' routine (which merely inspires an urgent desire to give the comforter a good slap). Time and again I felt it would have been easier to have broken a leg or gone down with pneumonia. Then I would have received practical, unembarrassed sympathy and support from everyone, not just a sensible few.

From *Song of the Spinning Sun* by Mary Frances

Emotional content also includes what other people were feeling about situations, whether these are family related, on a national scale or even worldwide. However, you can only include it if you truly know what they were feeling, otherwise you should let the reader know that you are hazarding a guess.

Verbal colour

Just as in writing a magazine article, although you will be getting rid of purple prose, you will need to add some verbal colour. The best adjectives are those which come from verbs, for example, 'He had dancing eyebrows' creates a stronger picture than 'He had eyebrows which moved up and down'.

Replace action verbs, which have been qualified with an adverb, with those which create a strong image on their own. For example, replace 'ran quickly' with 'rushed' or 'raced' and 'walked slowly' with 'sauntered' or 'wandered'.

Senses

Have you incorporated:

- Sound: such as your wedding bells, your baby's first cry, the crack of a cricket ball on a bat or the whoosh of skis over snow?
- Smell: such as seaweed, furniture polish or sun cream in a Spanish airport?
- Taste: such as bread, fresh from a brick oven, candyfloss or your first fresh pineapple?
- Touch: such as the roughness of sand in your shoes, the sting of lemonade bubbles in your nose or the silky feel of water in a woodland pool?

Characterization

When writing about family members and friends, as well as describing them physically, have you caught their foibles and eccentricities along with their funny habits and speech patterns?

Reflections

Looking back over your life you may want to add your thoughts and feelings about what has happened to you when viewed from a distance in time. Your readers will be interested to know about any regrets you may have or whether, had circumstances been different, you would have gone down a different route.

You might also want to compare and contrast what it was like during the various periods of your life with modern times and circumstances.

If you have any pearls of wisdom or advice to pass on then perhaps a summing up at the end of your manuscript is a good place to include them.

Voice

If you find that your voice has changed during writing your first draft, choose the style you feel most comfortable with and re-write the rest to match.

Last read-through

When you have made all your alterations and additions there are a few final checks to make:

- favourite words and sayings
- sentences
- spelling and punctuation
- names, dates and statistics.

Favourite words and sayings

We all have these and they are part of our voice, but overuse in your life story could get tedious to the reader so if you have used them too often take most of them out.

Sentences

Do some of the sentences leap out at you as being cumbersome? Are some too short and others too long? It is better to write short sentences rather than lengthy ones, but it is a good idea to have a variety of lengths.

A good rule of thumb is the more dynamic or exciting the action the shorter the sentences should be.

If a sentence seems a bit ploddy, it could be because you have used the passive form of the verb rather than the active one (see Chapter 13).

Spelling and punctuation

If you are writing on a computer you will be able to use the spellchecker. But this is not infallible because the word you have misspelt may also be a word in its own right, for example, 'meet' and 'meat'.

Check your punctuation and if you have over indulged in the use of exclamation marks now is a good time to delete some.

If you want to refresh your memory on when to use dashes or where to put apostrophes etc., turn to Chapter 13. There is also a section in this chapter which shows you how to check the readability of your manuscript.

Names, dates and statistics

Now is the time to double-check these. If you get them wrong that will be the one thing that the reader will remember.

If in doubt – take it out

Now that you have read your manuscript through several times are you still happy with what your have included? Even if you are only going to make a few copies for family and friends, once it has been printed off and is passed round it is too late to have second thoughts.

If you have any doubts about what you have written: such as whether it will cause offence or upset someone, or if you are not entirely sure of your facts – then it might be best to take it out.

Illustrating your manuscript

This is usually done with photographs and no doubt you have collected several during the course of researching your material. All you have to do now is decide which ones to use and where.

Improving photos

Old photos can be dramatically improved, such as taking out scratch marks and stains or filling in missing sections, by using the cloning tool in a computer software programme. These can be downloaded, often quite cheaply, from the Internet. Or you could take your photo to a specialist to have it improved.

Taking new

If you have old photos of where you went to school, or work, or played sports etc., you might want to take new photos of those places to act as a comparison.

Also why not include copies of your drawings and paintings or poems and short stories you have written or even birth, marriage and death certificates as well as old theatre programmes etc.

In fact an alternative to writing your life story is to create it pictorially.

Pictorially

It is said a picture paints a thousand words, so why not create a pictorial record of your life. This is what retired teacher and organist Ian Henderson has done.

Case study

Naturally family photographs will form the basis of such an operation, but photographs of the places where you were born, where you lived, went to school and worked can be included. These can be specially taken, but it is often possible to find old postcards which show scenes as they were when you were there. Postcards don't only show places; several are now available reproducing official notices and adverts of the past and these can be very evocative.

Tickets and maps, especially if the route taken for a particular journey can be shown, add interest, and you could include pictures of the ships or trains on which you travelled.

If you are lucky enough to have had a mother who hoarded things, school reports and early examples of your creative work may still be available. If you grew up in World War II your identity card and ration book may still be extant. Then there are birth and marriage certificates, and other certificates commemorating achievements, which can be used to form part of the collection, either as originals or reduced-size photocopies.

A note of special events and important occasions, with programmes, advertisements and tickets, where available, help to bring out the highlights. In fact anything which you feel has been important or significant in your life.

Since family photographs in particular often do not come to light until another member of the extended family has died, it is important to be flexible and remember that this is a 'work in progress'. For this reason it has been found best to mount material on coloured A4 sheets which can be displayed in a loose leaf folder or lever arch file.

There is no limit to the amount of pictorial information which can be presented and as 'a picture speaks a thousand words' no lengthy descriptions are needed, perhaps just a date or word or two of explanation.

Ian Henderson

Choosing your title

Finally you need to give your manuscript a name. Many people use a working title as they write and then spend time thinking about what to call their life story when they have finished. For others the title will come straightaway.

Example:

My mother knew right from the start that her memoirs would be called *Not Another Girl* because she was one of three girls and her mother was one of eleven girls.

It doesn't matter at what point you decide on a title, the main thing is to choose one which has reader appeal and which reflects your story.

There are various types of title:

- quotations
- play on words
- alliteration
- descriptive
- humorous
- obscure.

Quotations

To resonate with the reader, the quotation needs to be instantly recognizable. The most popular come from the Bible and Shakespeare. Titles can also come from well-known songs, poems, sayings and catchphrases.

Examples:

James Herriot used lines from a well-known hymn for several of his books including *All Things Bright and Beautiful* and *All Creatures Great and Small*.

The quotation could also be a favourite family saying but it may need to be explained somewhere in the book because future generations may not understand its significance.

Play on words

This is a popular form of title and can either be based on the author's name or profession.

Examples:

Seventies film star Kenneth More called his *More or Less*, and chef Gordon Ramsay called his *Humble Pie*.

Alliteration

If your name lends itself to alliteration (where all the words start with the same letter) this is another popular choice.

Examples:

Mike's Memoirs or *Marley and Me* (which although not entirely grammatical makes a good title).

Descriptive

Here the title gives a good indication of the memoir's content.

Example:

Toni Maguire's *Don't Tell Mummy*, is a story of a young girl's sexual abuse by her father.

Humorous

Example:

Comedian Spike Milligan's called two of his *Adolph Hitler: My Part in his Downfall* and *Mussolini: His Part in my Downfall.*

Obscure

Sometimes the more obscure the title the more intriguing it becomes.

Example:

Bill Bryson has called his autobiography *The Life and Times of the Thunderbolt Kid.*

Final changes

Check back on the reasons for writing your life story, what kind you wanted to write and how it was going to be written, and assess whether you have achieved your goal. If it falls short try to pinpoint why and make the necessary changes. If it is different are you happy with it? If not then make the necessary changes. Better to do this now than always be slightly disappointed with the final result.

Second opinion

When you have finished your second draft you may want to show it to someone to get a second opinion. However, try to choose someone who can be objective and who understands how to judge good writing.

Family and friends may not be the best people for this because either they may say that everything you've done is brilliant or, perhaps worse, they may be hypercritical and suggest you stop altogether – either way this isn't helpful to you.

Letting go

No one has yet written the perfect book, there is always a sentence which could be re-phrased or paragraphs which could be moved round. But there comes a time when you will have to say 'It is finished.' So lay down your pen or turn off your computer – having made sure that you have saved your work and backed it up – and pat yourself on the back.

You have achieved what many have said they would like to do, but few have succeeded in completing – you have written a book. It is now time to decide what to do with it.

Work in progress

In her first draft my mother described the rooms in her house, including the kitchen and its range. In the second draft she started adding more detail: such as how she and her sisters used to put their socks and gloves in the range before rushing out of the house to school or work. Then she added more emotional contents such as the family's feelings at the time when one of her sisters caught diphtheria and was held in an isolation hospital for a few weeks.

> *We could only visit her on Sundays, which meant a six-mile walk there and six miles back, and when we got there we weren't allowed in but had to stand outside and talk to her through glass. This was hard on Mum and Dad who were unable to even give her a hug.*

Exercise

Check your first chapter.

Add more emotional content.

Decide on a title.

Summary

In this chapter you have learnt:

- how to illustrate your book
- how to create a pictorial life story
- how to choose a title.

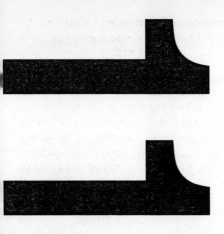

producing a page-turner

In this chapter you will learn:
- how to create reader curiosity
- when to use the present tense
- how to add humour.

We wouldn't be here if it wasn't for curiosity.

Jestyne Herbert

While family and friends will undoubtedly find your life story interesting it never hurts to add some more readability by taking a few tips from other writers. If you are aiming for publication, readability is essential.

How to fictionalize your life story is covered in Chapters 14 and 15, but in this chapter I am going to show you two ways of making your story a page-turner by adding curiosity and humour.

Curiosity

Basically there is only one thing that makes a reader turn the page – curiosity. In other words, they want to know what happens next. Depending on your genre, this could be an exciting cliffhanger, an impending tragedy or what you finally decided to wear to your daughter's wedding.

Creating curiosity is done in a variety of ways using:

- set-up
- foretaste
- foreshadowing
- suspense.

Set-up

As the heading suggests, this method is used at the start of chapters. Just as it was important to write a good opening paragraph in a magazine article so it is with your manuscript, but now you will need to write good opening paragraphs for each chapter.

Depending on the type of set-up, sometimes it can be accomplished in one paragraph or it might take several.

Top tip

The first paragraph of the first chapter is often the most difficult one to write, which is why, unless you know exactly what you are going to say, it might be better to leave it until last. It is worth spending a bit of time and trouble over it because this is where you are setting out your wares and saying to the reader 'come on in and read my book.'

There are several ways of writing a set-up including:

- flash forward
- present tense
- atmospheric
- intriguing or surprising
- realistic.

Flash forward

In this type of opening the writer describes the amazing, terrifying, exciting or amusing situation in which they find themselves. Once the writer has hooked the reader they then explain how they came to be in that situation and backtrack to fill in the missing information.

Example:

The professor's bloodshot eyes scanned the candidates. He leaned towards me. I could smell the whisky on his breath, I could see bits of grey stubble sneaking out of his red cheeks, I could feel his frustration. He continued in his inimitable rasping fashion: 'So you're telling me that none of you know what you would have done if one of your pupils wrote, "I ain't done nuffink wrong?"'

There was another tense silence. We shifted uneasily in our seats. All of us were at an interview that could possibly shape the rest of our lives. I had failed to get on any of the other teacher-training courses I had applied for because I had been far too bolshy and, though I would have normally voiced my views without a second thought, I drew breath here. In my estimation of things, a year of doing crappy, menial jobs in Brighton beckoned if I didn't get on this course.

**From *I'm a Teacher Get Me Out of Here*
by Francis Gilbert**

Present tense

Most life stories are written in the past tense but some writers use the present tense for the first one or two paragraphs – sometimes a whole chapter – to create a sense of immediacy in their writing. They then switch to the past tense.

This tense is sometimes used in conjunction with the flash forward.

Example:

I can hear a thud of hooves and heavy breathing – mine. I am riding Nobby, the greengrocer's pony, bareback and he is bolting with me. In the distance I can hear Wendy's plaintive wail, 'Stop galloping about, it's my turn to ride him.' I pull on the reins but the only effect that has is to pull me up his neck and into an even more precarious position.

Not for the first time I prayed: 'If I get off alive I'll never ride again.'

But I did, because when you are horse mad you ride anything which is offered to you, even Nobby. Who, to be fair, had got fed up with two young teenagers taking it in turns to ride him up and down the common.

Atmospheric

As well as setting the scene, this type of opening also creates an ambience whether one of peace and calm or chaos as in the example below. Like the above method it can pull the reader straight into the heart of the action.

Example:

The first thing we noticed as we docked at Singapore was a huge sign warning BEWARE OF THE SHARKS, but our minds were quickly diverted from the maritime dangers by one of the daily blanket raids by Japanese bombers on Keppel Harbour. We said our goodbyes to our generous USA hosts and disgorged ourselves from the ship in understandable haste.

From *Burma Railway, Images of War* by Jack Chalker

Intriguing or surprising

Intriguing first paragraphs can be written in several different ways but like the flash forward technique, once the writer has hooked the reader they then move into their life story proper.

Example:

On 23rd April 1978 at about five o'clock, I was a compass influenced by a million distracting metal parts. My needle veered haphazardly, pointing nowhere in particular. But at somewhere around two minutes past five I found magnetic North.

From *Song of the Spinning Sun* by Mary Frances

Realistic

Unlike the above example, this type of opening makes no bones about the writer's situation, but the reader is still curious to know how this situation came about and what the outcome will be.

Example:

I was born into a family of five children, a variety of dogs, two cats, one habitually violent father and a correspondingly nervous and frail mother. My father was a rag and bone man, my mother a 'gofer'. She seemed to spend her entire life running errands for neighbours, leaving little time to look after the home, or us. She would sacrifice anything and everything to help or please others. Often at the expense of her own children.

From *Unsettled* by Graham Walker

Top tip

Unless there is something unusual or significant about your birth it is probably better not to start your first paragraph with the words, 'I was born...' And don't start with an apology such as 'I'm afraid I'm not very good at writing, but I hope you find the following vaguely interesting' – the odds are the reader might not go any further.

Foretaste

This comes at the end of a chapter. It doesn't have to be on the scale of a blockbuster novel, but it does need to make the reader want to turn to the next chapter to find out what happens next.

Examples:

I was suddenly and immediately, with absolutely no effort whatsoever... free, anonymous, a lifetime's burdens lifted. I was free. I was alive. I WAS HOMELESS!

From *Unsettled* by Graham Walker

Or

On Valentine's Day I took my friend Maryrose's advice and gave myself two presents – a new car and a trip round the world.

From *Song of the Spinning Sun* by Mary Frances

Foreshadowing

This can come in the middle of a chapter where the writer feeds the reader a small piece of information, enough to whet their appetite, and then either writes something along the lines of: 'but more about that later' or switches to writing about something else.

Example:

While tidying the bureau I came across an unopened letter addressed to me, which I had never seen before. The return address appeared to be a solicitor's. However I didn't have time to open it as the doorbell rang – the washing machine engineer had arrived at last.

Suspense

Suspense is usually something associated with thrillers so unless you have led an exceptionally exciting life it may be difficult to achieve. However, it can be created by not revealing the outcome to a situation at the beginning – make the reader wait. The example below would not create any suspense if the writer had started the anecdote by explaining how lucky they were one dark night in Cornwall.

Example:

The scooter was practically out of petrol and we still had a long way to go before getting back to the hotel. We passed several petrol stations, but at 10 o'clock they were all closed for the night, after all it was Cornwall in the 1950s. The fuel gauge was registering empty. We were running on air and facing the prospect of spending the night at the side of the road, or pushing the Vespa some 20 miles.

'I only came out to give the dog a last walk,' said the owner of the petrol station as he filled up our tank. Luckily for us, as he had switched on the forecourt lights, a car, also nearly out of petrol, had pulled in and he had kindly served them. They were just about to pull away when we spluttered in. Once again he turned on the pumps and saved our day.

Closing paragraphs

Not all closing paragraphs have to be cliffhangers or give a foretaste, but they do have to round off the chapter.

Like those used in magazine articles, endings include:

- Closure: 'The furniture was still old and battered, but I no longer minded.'
- Making a statement: 'Nothing would ever be quite the same again.'
- Looking forwards: 'It was time to move on.'

Adding humour

Most life stories benefit from a touch of humour and it certainly adds readability. If you haven't already included some amusing incidents then look at some of your anecdotes – no matter how unfunny they seem – because you might be able to re-write them.

Comedy and tragedy are the two sides of the same coin. What makes a tragic situation appear humorous to the reader is because the author has written it in such a way as to invite the reader to laugh.

Example:

> *Looking for somewhere to sleep, I wandered around, fortunately stumbling across a large green bin with a swivel lid. Lighting a match, I happily discovered its contents contained some cardboard and bubble wrap. Enlisting my 'Blue Peter' mentality, I clambered into the bin and from the contents inside, made blankets and pillows which were surprisingly comfortable...*

> *Around 8 a.m., I was slowly roused by a low rumbling vibration. For a second or two, I just lay there, listening. Then it hit me. Crumbs! I was on the move! My God! I'm going to be compacted. I've gotta get out of here...*

From *Unsettled* by Graham Walker

The above example could be seen as a tragedy – having to sleep in a bin, nearly being crushed – but Graham allows us to laugh at his situation by the way he writes it. To write successful humour you need to be able to laugh at yourself.

Even in the most desperate of situations, the writer will
probably be able to include an amusing anecdote.

Example:

*Some months later, as I crept into my rice sacks one night,
I felt something run across my thigh and I grabbed it. It
was a scorpion and it slammed its pincers into my hand
and stung me with malevolent intent on the end of my
most private part. Within a few minutes it had swollen to
the size of a grapefruit and I was rolling about in agony,
unable to relieve the pain. The other occupants of the hut,
all of whom were heavy-sick, were hysterical with
laughter. A medical orderly covered in sores fetched the
MO, who on seeing me was also unable to contain his
laughter. As we were without medical supplies of any sort
all he could say was, 'Perhaps you had better put it in hot
water!' This bought the house down. It took days of
excruciating pain before I gained my normal function,
but the joke went on for years.*

From *Burma Railway, Images of War* by Jack Chalker

This anecdote works because the writer is prepared to tell a
story against himself.

The humorous life story

Including a few humorous anecdotes is one thing, but writing a
truly humorous life story is a different kettle of fish. You will
need to be the kind of person who always sees the funny side of
life and is prepared to find the comedy in virtually every
situation.

Of course, within this genre there are many different types of life
story. Some will be predominantly humorous, but with a few
sad or tragic episodes, while others will be relentlessly
humorous where every anecdote, even every sentence is written
to create a laugh.

They usually all begin with a good opening paragraph.

Example:

> *On 13 March, 1935, Hitler achieved air parity with Britain, Golden Miller won the Cheltenham Gold Cup for the fourth time, the Duke of Norfolk shot a rhino, and I reluctantly exchanged the comfort of my mother's womb for the uncertainty of life in Orpington.*

From I didn't get where I am Today by David Nobbs

On the face of it, this paragraph might appear to be breaking the principle of not starting your life story with your birth, but in this case David Nobbs has included it at the end of an eclectic list to create humour.

Endless books, and learned theses, have been written about humour and how to write humorously. This chapter can only touch on some of the basic principles which are:

- pain
- rule of three
- exaggeration
- incongruity
- rhythm and timing.

Pain

It is sad but true – we like to laugh at other people's pain. The clichéd joke about the man slipping on the banana skin makes us laugh because he is going to be in pain, albeit not much. The iconic moment in the sitcom *Fawlty Towers* where Basil is beating his car with a branch is all about pain (his, not the car's).

When writing a humorous life story it is mainly your pain that people will be laughing at so you need to find the 'banana skin' situations in your life and relate them in a way which shows your pain, but allows the reader to laugh. The two examples earlier are all about the writers' pain.

Rule of three

Humour always works better if comments come in threes, this allows the humour to build. If some comments are funnier than others then save the funniest one till last.

Example:

> *I was dogged by misprints. There was a man who went into hospital with a perforated dung. There was a young lady whose hubby was underwater swimming. A promotional piece about the Hippodrome Cinema was not enhanced by the information that it had opened in 1882 as a threat.*

> **From *I didn't get where I am Today* by David Nobbs**

The above is also another example of the writer showing his pain. In this case David Nobbs is allowing the reader to laugh at his embarrassment at being the victim of so many misprints.

You will be able to create even more humour if you can pull the three comments together with a fourth comment.

Example:

> *My warts had appeared during the summer of 1958, on my hands only, and Orpington Hospital had attempted to burn them off. It had been a fiasco. A doctor had now prescribed ointment, which had to be kept on all day, so it was necessary to cover the warts with sticking plaster. The ends of the plaster would come loose and wave in the Yorkshire wind.*

> *Another problem was that my nose would run, due to going in and out between overheated offices and the raw air of a Northern winter.*

> *A third problem was that most people spoke in a thick South Yorkshire accent which I found almost entirely impenetrable.*

> *I like to think that, apart from plasters blowing in the wind, a streaming nose and the fact that I had to ask people to repeat everything at least three times, I cut quite an impressive figure.*

> **From *I didn't get where I am Today* by David Nobbs**

Exaggeration

Merely describing an object, situation or event may not be terribly funny – but exaggerating it will create a picture in the reader's mind which will be funny.

Example:

I planted parsnips seeds as per instruction on the packet –
nothing. I planted more parsnips seeds as per advice on the
radio – still nothing. I scattered parsnip seeds to the wind not
caring whether they hit the damn soil or not – and they grew.
And they kept on growing until they were the size of small moon
rockets. One could have fed a family of eight for two months.

Note that this example also builds on the rule of three.

Exaggeration works even better if you can add alliteration to it.

Example:

What a voice! Commuters at Victoria could hear it – and we
were living in Vauxhall.

Or

What a voice! Commuters at Victoria could hear it – Victoria,
South Africa.

Incongruity

The lumping together of two discordant parts is the basis of a
lot of comedy. The incongruous parts can be statements or
sentences or just an inappropriate adjective.

Example:

Terrified grass.

Rhythm and timing

Although rhythm and timing are usually associated with telling
jokes, they are also important when writing humour. Use
punctuation such as dashes, brackets and exclamation to dictate
the rhythm and timing, and make sure the punchline is at the
end.

Example:

*You can imagine how proud I was when I saw my first
word in print, the very first word of my professional
career. Wrong! I wasn't proud at all. I was upset. It was
'Thives' – Thives who broke into the home of Mrs Emily
Braithwaite stole...*

From *I didn't get where I am Today* by David Nobbs

Read all different kinds of humorous life stories and try to analyze the author's techniques. But don't try to copy the way they write: use a style which comes naturally to you, otherwise it will come across to your reader as false.

Exercise

Re-write your opening paragraph.

Re-write the closing chapter.

Add some humour to an anecdote.

Summary

In this chapter you have learnt:

- how to use a flash forward
- how to write an intriguing first paragraph
- how to use the rule of three in humour.

12

those little extras

In this chapter you will learn:

- how to give your book a professional finish
- what prelims are
- what prelims to include.

A short saying often contains much wisdom.

Sophocles

Once you have finished your final draft it is time to write all the extra pages which go to make up a book. If you look at any book you will see that it doesn't start with the main body of text, but includes several pages at the beginning, each one containing additional information: these are called the preliminary pages or prelims.

There are also final pages at the end of the book which also give more information.

Of course you don't have to include all of these pages, or even any of them. However, if you are planning to self publish (see Chapter 18) they will give your book a professional finish. If you are planning to do home publishing (see Chapter 19) you will probably want to include at least some of them. Should you find a traditional publisher to take it on they will want at least some of this information.

Prelims

Generally speaking these pages are either not numbered at all or have a different numbering system from the main body of the book, such as Roman numerals or letters.

Starting from the front of the book they are:

Biography

The first right-hand page sometimes contains a short biography of the writer. This can also go on the back cover instead.

Also by

If this is not your first book, then the reverse of the biography page will list your previous publications.

Frontispiece

Some books include a photo or some other illustration on the left-hand page facing the title page.

Title page

This is on the right-hand side and has the title, the subtitle and usually the author's name. Sometimes the publisher's name is shown at the bottom.

Reverse of title page

This carries all the publishing information. This includes the publisher's name, the date it was published, its International Standard Book Number (ISBN – a 13-digit code unique to each book), a paragraph on protecting the rights of the book against all kinds of reproduction and an assertion of the author's copyright. Sometimes it also has the name of the typesetter and the printer.

Contents

This is a list of the chapter titles and their page numbers. Depending on the type of life story, each chapter can have subheadings, showing what information is included. Sometimes this is placed after the dedication and acknowledgements pages.

List of illustrations

If you have included photos, maps or other illustrations then it is usual to list them and give page numbers. This is also the place to acknowledge the copyright and who owns the photos. If you have not been able to establish who owns the copyright to any illustrations you have used, this is a good place to indicate this and ask for any readers who do own it to contact you. Sometimes the list of illustrations is put at the back of the book.

Dedication page

This is not always included and sometimes dedications are put on the reverse of the title page along with the publishing information. However, dedicating your book to friends or family members is a nice way of saying thank you for putting up with any disruptions while you completed your book.

Acknowledgements

This is where you can say thank you to all those who helped you with your book. These can also be put on the same page as the dedications. Sometimes they appear at the end of a book.

Subscribers

If you are paying to have your book published from subscriptions you might want to list the subscribers' names as a way of acknowledging their support. Again, depending on space these could go with the dedications and acknowledgement.

> **Top tip**
>
> If you decide to name people who have either helped with the book or subscribed towards it, make certain you include everyone! Otherwise a general thank you might be more diplomatic.

Quotation if used

Some writers like to use a quotation to set the tone of the book.

Foreword

This is usually written by someone with either the necessary expertise or authority, endorsing your work.

Preface or introduction

This is an explanation or description of the book by the author. It can also include how it came to be written and what efforts were involved. Sometimes it ends with the date the book was completed, as opposed to published, and where it was written. This page can also include the acknowledgments rather than showing them on a separate page.

Final pages

Not all books have final pages but they can include:

Epilogue or conclusion

Memoirs which cover a period of the writer's life sometimes include an epilogue or conclusion to bring events up to date, or as a form of closure.

Appendices

These can be a useful way of including information which is useful to the reader, but which would have spoilt the flow of the memoirs if it had been included in the main body of text.

Example:

David Beckham's autobiography, *My Side*, includes a list of career records.

Bibliography

This is a list of books and publications which were read during the course of your research. They should be listed in alphabetical order by the surname of the author. After the surname put the author's first name, followed by the title of the book which is either underlined or italicized, followed by the name of the publisher and finally the date, or dates, of publication. Some bibliographies show the author's surname in capitals and other put the author's names in bold.

You can also include a list of websites in the bibliography or show them separately. At the time of writing there is no formal way of listing them. In this book they are shown in chapter order.

End notes

Writers who want to expand on a subject, but don't want to do this in the main body of the text indicate this by inserting a number in the text. These numbers are then listed at the end of the book with the expanded explanation.

Glossary

If your memoirs use specialist words such as sporting terms, scientific jargon or foreign words (if you are writing about living abroad), it is helpful to your readers if you include a glossary. This is like a dictionary and explains what these words mean. The words are listed in alphabetical order and can be printed in bold.

Index

This is a list of important words with the numbers of the pages on which they can be found. They can be names of people, places or concepts.

Summary

In this chapter you have learnt:

- how to number prelims
- how to write a bibliography
- how to write a glossary.

13

grammar

In this chapter you will learn:

- basic grammar
- how to punctuate
- how to avoid common errors.

I don't give a damn for a man that can only spell a word one way.

Mark Twain

Many people worry that their grammatical skills aren't good enough to write a book, but there is no need – after all you don't give grammar a thought when you are talking to people so you must know some of the basic rules already.

Put at their simplest, grammar and punctuation are just systems for making writing easier for the reader to understand. If you picked up a book which was just a mass of words with no sentences, paragraphs, full stops or commas, you would probably put it straight back down because it would be too difficult to make any sense out of it.

Language is made up from words – in the English language there are thousands, possibly more than a million, no one really knows. However, these are the tools we work with.

Sentences

A sentence is a group of words which can stand alone and be understood. A simple sentence contains one statement. Example: *I am going to write my life story*.

However, a book which is written entirely in simple sentences would be uninteresting to read and you should aim to have a mixture of simple and compound sentences.

Compound sentences are made up from simple statements and/or sub clauses. There are various ways of creating them:

- using conjunctions or joining words such as 'and' or 'but'
- using commas
- using semicolons.

Using conjunctions

Example: *I am going to write my memoirs and I hope to have them finished in three months' time*. The conjunction 'and' joins two statements.

Using commas

Commas can be used to join two statements or to indicate an addition. (For more on additions see below under 'Commas'.)

Example: *I am going to write my memoirs, they shouldn't take long.* The comma joins two statements which could stand alone.

I am going to write my memoirs, hopefully. 'Hopefully' is an addition to the sentence.

Using semicolons

Example: *I am going to write my memoirs; they will start at my birth and continue to the present day.*

> **Top tip**
> Use simple sentences when the statement makes an impact on its own. Example: *I am going to write my memoirs.* Use compound sentences to add colour and description to your writing.

The way you create these compound sentences will often be a matter of personal choice, and will reflect your own style of writing. The order in which sentence are written, particularly those which contain one or more sub clauses, will also reflect your personal style.

Example: *My memoirs, which will be full of racy comment and salacious gossip, will reveal just what goes on when the curtain goes down.*

This could also be written: *Full of racy comment and salacious gossip, my memoirs will reveal just what goes on when the curtain goes down.*

Paragraphs

Paragraphs are made up from one or more sentences which all relate to one topic or theme. Ideally each paragraph should have a key sentence which sums up what the theme of the paragraph is about. Usually it is the first sentence but it does not have to be. The rest of the sentences amplify or add evidence to the topic or theme. The last sentence should also make you want to read on.

Example: *Full of racy comment and salacious gossip, my memoirs will reveal just what goes on when the curtain goes down. Having spent many years in show business, I am privy to many secrets about household names. Secrets they would prefer remained untold.*

The first sentence indicates the theme and the last sentence ends the paragraph in a tantalizing way.

Transitions

Sometimes called link words, they link clauses within a sentence, sentences within a paragraph and paragraphs within a book.

See Chapter 06 for an example of transitions.

Basic punctuation

These help to clarify the sense of what has been written.

Full stops

These are easy – they come at the end of a sentence. They are replaced by question marks if the sentence is a question.

Commas

These have several important uses which include:

- separating words in lists
- separating extra information
- marking additions
- indicating a brief pause
- affecting the meaning
- marking dialogue.

Separating words in a list

This is one of the most common uses. They are also used to separate a list of phrases.

Example: *What I like most is sitting in a hot tub, drinking champagne, eating strawberries and reading my diary.*

Separating extra information

Use a comma either side of an additional piece of information.

Example: *The stagehand, who had only recently joined the company, helped me carry my shopping up to the dressing room.*

The sentence would still make sense if the additional information is left out: *The stage hand helped me carry my shopping up to the dressing room.*

Marking additions

These include phrases such as 'I believe' and 'thank you', linking phrases such as 'however' and 'on the other hand', and people's names.

Example: *The leading man, John Smith, played his part to perfection. The same, however, could not be said for the leading lady.*

> **Top tip**
> Don't forget the second comma when putting additional information in a sentence.

Indicating a brief pause

When we are talking we naturally add pauses to our speech patterns. By using commas to break up long sentences into smaller segments, we make them easier to read, and we also indicate where to take a brief pause.

> **Top tip**
> Read your writing aloud and where you pause naturally, put in a comma.

Affecting the meaning

The English language is full of ambiguities but one way of ensuring that the reader understands what you are writing is by the correct use of commas.

Example: *To help raise money for the theatre she runs trips, and bakes cakes as well.*

But if the comma is put after 'runs' the meaning is completely changed: *To help raise money for the theatre she runs, trips, and bakes cakes as well.*

For more on ambiguities see Chapter 06.

Marking dialogue

Put a comma after the person speaking and inside the speech marks if the speech is broken.

Example: *'Rain before seven,' said my mother, 'dry before eleven.'*

> **Top tip**
> Don't overuse commas and spoil the flow of your writing.

Apostrophes

Apostrophes are tiny marks on the page but probably cause more problems than the rest of punctuation put together. They perform two functions:

- to show possession
- to indicate missing letters.

To show possession

Example: *The actor's dressing room was bigger than mine.*

Because the actor is singular the apostrophe goes before the 's'. If there is more than one actor the apostrophe goes after the 's': *The other actors' dressing rooms were bigger than mine.*

Time is also possessive and the same rules for singular and plural apply.

Example: *In one year's time I shall be nine. In ten years' time I shall be 18.*

Where names already end in 's' you have a choice of whether to put an extra 's' after the apostrophe or leave it out – a good guide is to say the word aloud and punctuate accordingly.

Example: *David Nobbs' novels* or *David Nobbs's novels.*

If you're not comfortable with either construction in your life story re-write the sentence and use 'of' or 'belonging to'.

Some plurals are not formed by adding an 's'. To show possession for these words treat them as singular and put the 's' after the apostrophe. As in *Children's books.*

To indicate missing letters

When words are shortened or contracted the apostrophe replaces the missing letters.

Example: *Can't* = cannot, *They're* = they are, *It's* = it is

One of the main errors in writing is when to use 'it's' and 'its'. '*Its*' is a possessive pronoun in the same way as '*mine*', '*yours*' and '*theirs*', so, like them, it doesn't need an apostrophe.

Example: *The play ran its course.* In this case 'its' is the possessive pronoun and doesn't need an apostrophe.

It's time to bring down the curtain. In this case 'It's is a shortened version of 'It is' so does need the apostrophe to indicate the missing letter.

Inverted commas

These are also known as speech marks, quotation marks or quotes and are used to enclose:

- direct speech
- quotations
- book, play or song titles.

It is a matter of choice whether you use single or double inverted commas, but be consistent throughout your writing.

Direct speech

Example: *The director said, 'Sorry, darling, you are doing it all wrong, I need more emotion.'*

Quotations

Indicate a quote within a direct speech with double inverted commas if the speech is in single ones and vice versa.

Example: *I replied, 'Don't say to me "I need more emotion", tell that to the others.'*

Quotations taken from other sources are also enclosed in inverted commas. If the quote is a sentence, then put a full stop inside the inverted commas, if it is just a phrase, put the full stop outside. Very common short quotes from well-known writers or the Bible don't need quote marks.

When using passages from something written by someone else remember that there are limits to how much you can quote (see Chapter 04 for fair dealing).

Book, play or song titles

These have inverted commas either side.

Example: 'Teach Yourself Writing a Play'.

Although you could write your memoirs using only the basic punctuation marks outlined above, it will add colour and interest if you use some of the following as well.

Exclamation marks

These are used instead of full stops to indicate:

• strong emotions e.g. *I couldn't believe my ears!*
• exclamatory phrases e.g. *How stupid can you get!*

Some writers develop the habit of using them to signal a joke or light-hearted remark.

Example: *I fell off the stage, twisted my ankle, dropped my script and broke my mobile phone. It just wasn't my day!*

They are also used to signal to the reader that a remark is not meant to be taken seriously.

Example: *The director singled me out for praise. I was so embarrassed I could have murdered him!*

Although exclamation marks can add colour to your writing, use them sparingly!

Semicolons

As well as joining statements, semicolons can also be used to separate lists, particularly where the lists are complicated by additional descriptions.

Example: *What I like most is sitting in a hot tub, preferably on my balcony; drinking champagne, which must be iced; eating strawberries, which must be fresh from Somerset and reading my diary.*

Colons

Colons are used before lists.

Example: *I always travelled with my own tea-making equipment: a samovar, tea bags and a porcelain bowl.*

And before explanations.

Example: *I always travelled with my own tea making equipment: one could never be certain what facilities would be available in the dressing room.*

Dashes

These can be used instead of colons and semi-colons to make a sentence more dramatic.

Example: *Furious, I raised myself up to my full height and looked the director in the eye – this time I was going to speak my mind.*

They can also indicate that that what follows will be unexpected or surprising in some way.

Example: *Furious, I raised myself up to my full height and looked the director in the eye – or rather his chest.*

Used in this way they give writing a racier more colloquial feel, but, like exclamation marks, use them sparingly.

They can also be used instead of commas either side of a piece of additional information to give it more impact.

Example: *The director – he of the lime green kimono and jodhpurs – sat down beside me in the stalls and commiserated.*

Brackets

These are used on either side of additional information, where they can have the effect of diminishing the impact.

Example: *The director (a tall, handsome man) sat down beside me in the stalls and introduced himself.*

Or either side of explanations.

Example: *I then spent a wretched season in pantomime (read more about this in Chapter 38).*

Or

My finest hours were spent with the RSC (The Royal Shakespeare Company) where my talents were fully recognized.

Ellipsis

An ellipsis is a row of three dots. It is mostly used in quotes to indicate that not all the quote has been used, only the relevant parts – however you shouldn't use this to distort the writer's meaning.

Example: *In* Teach Yourself Writing for Magazines, *the author says that 'using dashes... gives writing a racier more colloquial feel.'*

It can also be used to imply words which are not actually written down.

Example: *After revealing her true feelings for me, my leading lady and I left the stage door together...*

Some writers also use an ellipsis instead of a dash to create a longer pause.

Example: *After a severe bout of laryngitis, calls for my sonorous bass tones for voice-overs tailed off... well if truth be told they disappeared entirely.*

Hyphens

These little dashes, which join prefixes to words or words together in a group, can cause confusion because words which were once hyphenated now aren't. For example: *co-operative* is now usually written *cooperative*.

They are still used between numbers such as *thirty-three*, *40-year-old man,* compound adjectives such as *shop-made,* and phrases such as *world-war-one veteran.*

Active and passive verbs

Verbs have an active and a passive form. With the active form the subject of the sentence carries out the action: *The director saved the dog from drowning.* Here 'the director' is the subject of the sentence and it is he who carries out the action.

With the passive form the subject of the sentence is the recipient of the action: *The dog was saved from drowning by the director.* Here 'the dog' is the subject and has the saving done to it by *the director.*

As you can see, the active form is more dynamic and the emphasis is on the positive action of the subject. In the passive version, not only is the sentence longer, but the emphasis is on the negative action of the subject, in other words the dog did nothing towards saving itself.

In the majority if cases, therefore, it is preferable to use the active form. The only time that you would choose to use the passive form is when the recipient of the action is of more interest to the reader than the person doing the action: *The leading lady was saved from drowning by the director.* In this case the leading lady is of more interest than the person who saved her.

Action verbs

These are also sometimes referred to as active verbs, which can be confusing in light of the above. However, they are descriptive verbs which give the reader extra information. For example: *shimmying, waltzing or jiving* gives more information to the reader than *dancing*. Similarly, *warbling, crooning or chanting* says more than *singing*.

Spelling

This is also a big worry to writers – and with reason because English spelling doesn't always follow any rules.

If you are using a computer then the spellchecker certainly helps, but their weakness is that they don't pick up on mistakes which are also words.

Top tip
Don't forget to set the spellchecker to UK English.

There are ways to improve your spelling:

- Always have a dictionary handy and use it even if you think you might be right.
- Make a list of words you constantly get wrong and try to learn to spell them correctly.
- Use memory aids with words you find difficult.

Words which confuse

These fall into three categories:

- similar sounding words
- easy mistakes
- common mistakes.

Similar sounding words

Adverse means 'unfavourable' and *averse* means 'disinclined'.

Affect means 'to act on' or 'change' and *effect* means 'to bring about'.

Aural relates to hearing and *oral* relates to speaking.

Compliment means 'an expression of praise' and *complement* means 'an addition to'.

Council means 'an assembly' and *counsel* means 'giving advice or a barrister'.

Councillor means 'a member of an assembly' and *counsellor* means 'a person who gives advice'.

Current means 'in the immediate present' and *currant* means 'a dried fruit'.

Discreet means 'keeps a confidence or is unobtrusive' and *discrete* means 'separate or distinct'.

Disinterested means 'impartial' and *uninterested* means 'having no personal interest'.

Elicit means 'to bring to light' and *illicit* means 'illegal'.

Especially is used when describing something unusual or notable and *specially* is used when describing something for a particular purpose.

License is the verb meaning 'to grant' and *licence* is the 'certificate' given when licensed.

Practice means 'something which is customary or usual' and *practise* means 'to repeat an action to gain a skill'.

Principal means 'someone or something ranked first' and *principle* means 'a rule or code of conduct'.

Stationary means 'not moving' and *stationery* means 'writing materials'.

Easy mistakes

Using:

- *there's* instead of *theirs*
- *who's* instead of *whose*
- *you're* instead of *your*
- *your's* instead of *yours*.

Common mistakes

- *bored **with*** not *bored of*
- *different **from*** not *different than* or *different to*
- *fed up **with*** not *fed up of*
- *try **to*** not *try and*.

Journalistic conventions

There are certain journalistic conventions which dictate how numbers are written. Generally speaking they are written in the following way but check the house style to be on the safe side.

Numbers one to nine are written as words, 10 and over are written as numbers except when they start a sentence. However, don't mix words and numbers in the same phrase, use numbers. (Note: house style for *Teach Yourself* dictates that numbers one to ten be written as words and 11 and over be written as numbers. Subsequently, this is the tack taken in this book.)

Percentages: Check whether the magazine uses the percentage sign % or writes it out as in full 'per cent'.

Fractions: Check whether to write 1/3 or 'one-third'.

Dates: These can be written with dashes '2002–2008', or 'between 2002 and 2008', or 'from 2002 to 2008'.

Measuring readability

There are various ways of measuring the readability of a piece of writing.

The Gunning Fog Index measures the average number of words in a sentence and adds the percentage of words with three or more syllables. The resulting figure is the number of years of education a reader would need in order to be able to understand the piece. Writing that uses short words and short sentences will have a lower score than writing that uses long words and long sentences. A Gunning Fog index of below ten is desirable for most articles.

There is software available for measuring the Gunning Fox Index, but some versions of Microsoft Word will also measure the readability of writing. Click on 'tools', then on 'spelling and grammar'. Check the article sentence by sentence and at the end an information box will come up giving the statistics. The important ones are:

- Words per sentence – Check this against the house style of your chosen magazine.
- Passive sentences – The fewer there are the better.
- Flesch Reading Ease – It rates text out of 100, the higher the score the easier it is to understand the writing. Aim for between 60 and 70.

• Flesch-Kincaid Grade Level – This is similar to the Gunning Fox Index in that it measures the educational level of the reader. Aim for a level around 8.

Summary

In this chapter you have learnt:

• to avoid ambiguities
• some journalistic conventions
• how to measure readability.

section three

three
fictionalizing
your life
story

14

how a novel works

In this chapter you will learn:
- how to use conflict
- how to use the dramatic arc
- how to create dialogue.

The most important element in writing good fiction is to become your own best editor. Techniques such as characterization, story structure, 'show, not tell' and pacing are all vital, but the most vital ingredient of all is to be able to read your work as if it was written by someone else – and adjust accordingly.

Lee Weatherly, author of *Teach Yourself How to Write a Blockbuster*

In Chapter 11 I suggested two ways of giving your life story more readability. However, if you want to fictionalize your life story – whether it be writing it in a novelistic form or using it as a basis for a novel – it is a good idea to have some understanding of how novels work.

Novels are basically stories, and the art of storytelling goes back into the mists of time, before reading and writing. Most novels follow the well-established conventions of storytelling.

Of course there will always be successful writers who go their own way, but if you are a first-time writer it might be safer if you to stick to the tried and trusted route. And if you intend to ignore the conventions, then first you will need to understand what you are going to ignore.

However, there is a fine line between following the rules and writing by numbers. The former will give your story an underlying structure without impinging on your style, the latter will come across as formulaic and stilted.

Many writers already have an inbuilt understanding of the conventions, others learn how to use them by reading a wide variety of novels, but most of us need a bit of extra help.

If writing your life story to a format all sounds a bit prescriptive, don't worry, it isn't. Just write the first draft and then check to see that all the parts are in place.

Conflict

Without conflict there is no story – or rather there is no story that anyone will want to read because without conflict nothing of interest happens.

However, the word 'conflict' in storytelling doesn't mean fighting with the neighbours or arguing with the family – although these may be included in your book – it is how you and the other characters in your story find yourselves thwarted or opposed in getting what you want. The more extreme your desire, the more opposition put in your way – the more dramatic possibilities there are in the story.

And the level of conflict needs to increase as the storyline unfolds, building towards the moment of crisis where it looks as though all is lost.

But conflict in a life story does not have to be on a grand scale like a blockbuster, a chapter could be written about how the main character, or protagonist as they are generally referred to in novelistic terms, is continually thwarted while trying to buy a pair of shoelaces.

Conflict operates on three levels:

- internal conflict
- interpersonal conflict
- external conflict.

Internal conflict

This is where the protagonist is being thwarted by themselves. Perhaps they are struggling with their inner demons. Perhaps they know what they should be doing to achieve success but are too lazy to carry out the necessary steps.

In *Pride and Prejudice* by Jane Austen, the title indicates where the internal conflict comes from. In the case of the protagonist, Elizabeth Bennett, she is prejudiced against Darcy because of his proud behaviour, and her pride causes her to reject his proposal of marriage. The same also applies to Darcy.

Interpersonal conflict

This is the most common type of conflict in a novel and is where the protagonist is thwarted or opposed by others – and in the context of a novel, others can be animals, inanimate objects and forces of nature as well as people.

Elizabeth is in conflict with Darcy, blaming him for preventing Bingley and Jane from becoming engaged, and for a while she is thwarted from making a suitable marriage by her younger sister Lydia's elopement.

External conflict

Here, the protagonist is in conflict with society at large, whether it is faceless bureaucracy or unfair laws.

Elizabeth is in conflict with her culture, which requires girls to make the most advantageous marriage they can. When Mr Collins proposes she knows that by accepting him she could save her whole family from losing everything when her father dies.

If we look at our character who is trying to buy a pair of shoelaces his internal conflict could come from his being too lazy to set his alarm clock causing him to over-sleep. This means he gets caught in a traffic jam and can't find anywhere to park. The interpersonal conflict comes from trying to jam his car into too small a space and hitting the car behind. This puts him in conflict with the space, the other car and probably the other driver. The external conflict comes from not buying a parking ticket and receiving a penalty ticket from a traffic warden.

Dramatic arc

Dramatic arc doesn't mean your book has to be about high drama or hair-raising adventures – although it could be – it is just a term to describe the logical pattern of the story.

The parts of a dramatic arc are:

- set-up
- trigger – sometimes called the inciting moment
- obstacles, including twists and reverses
- crisis
- climax
- resolution or pay-off
- ending.

Set-up

In the previous chapter we talked about using the set-up as a way of producing curiosity and when it comes to fictionalizing your life story this will still apply. Jane Austen starts *Pride and Prejudice* with a sentence which is intriguing, but also hints at the storyline:

> *It is a truth universally acknowledged, that a single man in possession of a good fortune, must be in want of a wife.*

The length of the set-up will depend on the type of novel. If the setting of your novel is going to play an important part such as in Karen von Blixen's *Out of Africa* then the set-up could be quite long.

It may seem obvious, but all stories have a beginning and where you start them is very important. If your story is character driven, then you will probably start with the main protagonist (which will most likely be you), who, if not at peace with the world, is at least getting on with life. If you are writing your life story as an adventure novel then you should begin as close to the trigger point as possible (see below). In fact some writers like to start at the trigger point and then fill in the back story afterwards. This is the same as the flash forward technique described in Chapter 11, but may last longer.

Trigger

Also known as the Inciting Incident, this is the most important point in the novel: it is the moment when the storyline springs into action, the characters come alive and nothing will be the same until the final resolution. In other words it is the start of the quest: because all stories are ultimately a quest.

The trigger can be an external force over which the protagonist has no control, or it can be a situation which has been activated by some flaw in their character. It may be a major event, or something so insignificant that it is not recognized as such until some time later. However, it is the protagonist's reaction to this event and the decisions they take, which sets in motion the rest of the story.

In *Pride and Prejudice* there is quite a long set-up, but the trigger which sets the story in motion is the moment when Mr Bingley arrives in the locality and is known to have a large fortune.

> **Top tip**
> If you have more than one choice for your trigger, try to pick the most dramatic one.

Motivation

To get the protagonist to react to the trigger there has to be motivation. This can be a response to human needs or be entirely altruistic. In *Pride and Prejudice* the motivation is the need to marry well. When a soldier goes to rescue a fellow comrade under fire the motivation is altruistic.

Obstacles

Once the trigger has been introduced then the story needs a series of obstacles which have to be overcome by the protagonist – or there would be no story. Like conflict, these don't have to be death-defying, their nature will depend on the type of novel, but they do need to be there. Again, like conflict these obstacles can be the result of outside forces or, even better, as a result of the protagonist's own character flaws. In *Pride and Prejudice* Elizabeth comes to realize that her embarrassing family is an obstacle preventing her and Jane from marrying well.

Twists

Another way of creating obstacles, and to keep the reader guessing, is to introduce a twist. If you are turning your life story into an adventure story it will certainly benefit from one or more.

They can be added in various ways such as introducing a new character or revealing an unexpected piece of information. In *Pride and Prejudice* the arrival of Mr Wickham ensures Elizabeth is attracted to him rather than Darcy. Wickham also reveals information that he has been badly treated by Darcy confirming Elizabeth's prejudice against him.

Reversals

These are similar to twists but completely reverse a situation. A character who the reader believes is a hero is shown to be the villain or vice versa. Wickham is shown to be a seducer and Elizabeth's decision not to make this known to her family has dire results for them.

Crisis

This is the biggest obstacle of all and must appear insurmountable. Once Elizabeth's sister Lydia is seduced by Wickham, Elizabeth believes that neither she nor Jane will ever be able to make a suitable marriage. It is only when Darcy persuades Wickham to marry Lydia in return for money that the crisis passes.

Climax

The highest point of the dramatic arc is the climax. The protagonist faces their biggest challenge and either wins or loses depending on the story. For Elizabeth the climax is the visit from

Lady Catherine who, knowing about Lydia's seduction, insists that Elizabeth must never become engaged to Darcy. Elizabeth refuses to give an undertaking which would be against her own happiness: a courageous action to take in a culture where someone from a lower class would be expected to give way to a person from a higher class.

Resolution or payoff

The quest is over and the goal is in sight. It is more satisfying if the protagonist's own character traits enable them to win through. It is Elizabeth's stubbornness which wins the day because Darcy learns that she refused Lady Catherine's request and this gives him the courage to propose to her a second time.

Ending

Byron wrote: 'All tragedies end with a death and all comedies with a marriage.' That doesn't necessarily hold good for all novels, but there should be a definite outcome to the protagonist's difficulties.

However, creating a satisfying ending does need some thought. It shouldn't come as a bolt from the blue – on the other hand an element of surprise won't come amiss either. The main criterion is that it should follow inevitably from what has gone before, even if the reader doesn't realize what it will be until it actually happens.

In *Pride and Prejudice* the marriage of Elizabeth and Darcy is always going to be the obvious outcome, but other novels are equally satisfying if the protagonist doesn't achieve their goal, but acquires closure in some other way. In Thomas Hardy's *Tess of the D'Urbervilles* the main protagonist dies, but there is a real sense of closure to the story.

Subplots

Only short stories or very short novels don't have subplots. Subplots are developed around one or more of the other characters, and while they can be complete in themselves they do have an effect on the main plot. Even if at the beginning of a novel the subplots seem to be completely independent stories – a popular ploy in thriller writing – by the end they will converge.

Each subplot needs to follow its own dramatic arc. Also if you are writing your story as a series of episodes then each episode should follow the dramatic arc.

Dialogue

It is possible to write a novel without any dialogue, but most writers like to insert some to bring the characters to life.

Dialogue is not the same as conversation. Conversation happens in real life and it is often superficial, repetitive and sometimes rambling.

This means that although you will need to keep to the essence of a conversation between your characters, it will need to be shaped to perform one or more of three functions:

- revealing character
- moving the plot forward
- giving information.

How much you have to deviate away from what was actually said, or how much you will need to add, depends on which of these functions you are trying to achieve. It will also depend on whether you are fictionalizing your life story or making it a basis for a novel. If it is the former you may be limited to what changes you make to the dialogue. If it is the latter you will probably have more scope.

Revealing character

Hearing the characters speak creates an extra layer in the story. The old adage 'show don't tell' comes into play here. Rather than being told that a character has a nasty temper, or is as sweet as pie, let the reader see for themselves through the character's dialogue as well as their actions.

Moving the plot forward

Although not the main way of moving the plot forward, dialogue can be used, for example, if one character says something that upsets another, or when a character reveals a secret to another.

Giving information

This function needs to be used carefully because the writer needs to avoid having one character tell another one what the second one already knows. Sometimes it is easier for the writer to tell the reader this information.

Speech patterns

Each of the characters will have their own specific speech pattern such as the words and phrases they use. These can tell the reader quite a lot about them, for example, an impatient person will use short sentences and won't waste words.

Under pressure people change their speech patterns and often reveal perhaps their true nature, for example the bully when confronted by someone stronger than themselves will revert to abject pleading.

Regarding dialect, the same rules apply here as in writing a life story. Avoid phonetically spelling words in dialect, but indicate it by using one or two common phrases from that particular region. For example a Bristolian might say: 'Where's he to then?' instead of 'Where is he?' Sometimes all that is needed is a slight rearrangement of words in a sentence.

Practicalities

As well as the point above it is also necessary to take the following into account:

- Ensure that the reader knows who is speaking.
- Break dialogue up with action.
- If possible, give each speaker their own paragraph.
- While some replacements for the word 'said' such as 'cried', 'chuckled' or 'growled', help to indicate character or enhance a situation, overindulgence is irritating to the reader and probably unnecessary.
- Read it aloud to check that it sounds right.

Delaying information

As well as following the dramatic arc, there are other techniques which can be incorporated.

We've already looked at this in relation to writing a life story where the writer introduces a 'teaser' and then makes the reader wait for a page (or chapter) or two before explaining it. But when you fictionalize your life story you can keep the reader intrigued for longer by dangling a piece of information in front of them, but not explaining what it is. One way to do this is to switch to writing about a subplot.

> **Top tip**
> Feed information a little at a time.

Themes

These are different from both the plot and the story and are the basic principles which govern human behaviour such as: love, hate, fear, redemption, loss, power, self-delusion, gullibility.

In *Pride and Prejudice* the title again indicates the themes running through the work. And these themes are not confined to the protagonist or the main storyline, but occur in the subplots as well.

Some writers have a theme in mind before they start work on their novel, in fact they may use the same themes in more than one book. Others clarify it as the work progresses. Because you are turning work which already exists into a novel, its themes may not be readily recognizable, but once you start writing it is worth trying to analyze the themes running through it. While they won't influence its shape, they will underpin the story and give it coherence and the novel will work better if you cut out everything which does not conform to your theme.

Message

If your life story has a cathartic or therapeutic theme then you may well want it to give a message to the reader.

Whole books are written on how to write a novel so this chapter can only scratch the surface and give you a few hints. For more detailed information read *Teach Yourself How to Write a Blockbuster* or *Teach Yourself How to Write a Novel*.

Exercise

Analyze the conflict and the dramatic arc in a novel based on a life story.

Look at the incidents you plan to write about in your own life story. Where is the conflict? What is the dramatic arc?

Identify the trigger or inciting moment.

Summary

In this chapter you have learnt:

- about the different types of conflict
- the components of the dramatic arc
- how to use speech patterns.

15

turning your life story into a novel

In this chapter you will learn:
- how to use the novelistic form
- how to write your life story as a novel
- the difference between plot and story.

> *Readers of true-life stories are attracted by the same elements that draw them to any other story – drama, excitement, romance, humour. If you can inject these qualities into your account, you'll hook them.*
>
> **Scott Mariani, tutor, Writers' News course, 'Making the most of your life experiences'**

There is a long tradition of fictionalizing life stories, which are sometimes called autobiographical novels, and there are two basic ways of doing it:

- writing them in a novelistic form
- using them as a basis for a novel or short story.

But inevitably there will be books which fall in between these two categories.

Novelistic form

Although they may appear to be a normal life story, written in the first person and past tense, the main differences of those written in a novelistic form are:

- They have been adapted to comply with the dramatic arc. For example, Monica Dickens' books *One Pair of Hands*, *My Turn to Make the Tea* and *One pair of Feet* which are about her experiences as a cook, cub reporter and nurse, or Andy McNab's *Bravo Two Zero,* a page-turning adventure book about his experiences in the Gulf War.
- The characters and/or the writer may have been disguised. For example, James Herriot's books on his veterinary experiences were not written under his real name. Andy McNab is not the real name of the author of *Bravo Two Zero* and Francis Gilbert, who wrote *I'm a Teacher Get Me Out of Here,* says at the beginning of his book that the characters are composites and made up, but the stories are based on real incidents.

Another way of writing in a novelistic manner is by using episodic chapters. Each chapter will have a self-contained story following the dramatic arc (see Chapter 14). However they should all be connected to each other in some way either by a time span, such as stories of your childhood, or a change of direction such as starting a new career or moving abroad, or a theme such as anniversaries.

Examples:

Most of the chapters in James Herriot's *Vets Might Fly* are recollections of incidents in his Yorkshire veterinary practice. These are triggered by something which is happening during his initial training in the RAF. Although each chapter is a self-contained story, they are pulled together by confining them to a time span: the period from call up to going to flying school, and a change of direction: suddenly finding himself in the armed forces.

The 12 chapters in Peter Mayle's *A Year in Provence* are connected by time, because they are based on the 12 months in one year, but also by a theme, that of renovating a farmhouse.

Of course, not all books in this genre are written in the first person: Flora Thompson's books *Lark Rise, Over to Candleford* and *Candleford Green*, based on her experiences as a young child, are written in the third person.

Not all life stories will lend themselves to being fictionalized, but once again, it is well worth reading all different types of novels based on real life and analyzing how other writers have fictionalized their experiences – and whether you could do something similar.

Novel or short story

Most writers starting a novel from scratch would probably have to spend days or even months mulling over the storyline and where it will be set as well and getting to know their characters. You, of course, have a head start on the novelist because you already know all this – however it is likely you will have to make some adjustments to your life story so that it conforms to the conventions of a traditional novel.

To do this you may have to:

- restrict your dramatized version to a specific part of your life – you can always write other novels about the other parts
- cut out large chunks which hinder the action
- alter or add characters or make composites if you have too many
- choose a genre: such as romance, adventure, tragedy or thriller.

In Chapter 14 we looked at the basic structure of a novel: the dramatic arc. But that just provides the skeleton. You now have to graft on to that the components of a novel.

Novel components

There are plenty of good books and websites on how to write a novel. They sometimes differ on what is meant by plot, and whether it the same as the storyline and whether there is only one or seven or more universal storylines. I'm going to nail my colours to the mast and say, in the context of turning your life story into a novel, it needs:

- a plot
- a story
- characters
- a setting
- a viewpoint.

However don't take this as the definitive version: it's just my way of analyzing the novel. And although I have listed them in this order, it doesn't necessarily mean that the plot and storyline are more important than characters or setting. Depending on the type of novel, it could be character led or the setting may play the most important part.

Plot

We all instinctively feel we know what is meant by the word 'plot'. If someone asks us to describe the plot of a book such as Jane Austen's *Pride and Prejudice* we would probably answer that it is all about marrying off your daughters to men with money and position. Of course there are several subplots, but this is the main thrust of the book.

So how do you find the plot for your life story, or the section of it which you intend to write? One way is to try to describe the essence of your proposed novel in one sentence.

It may be that your plot doesn't become obvious until you have started writing, but once you have established what it is then you need to stick with it to stop your book going off in the wrong direction.

Imagine if Jane Austen, having decided her main plot is about the necessity for women to get married then changed direction

185
turning your life story
into a novel

15

halfway through the book and started writing about how much better it was to remain a spinster.

Story

The story puts flesh on the bare bones of the plot. In *Pride and Prejudice*, Jane Austen could have written an endless number of stories based on her plot, but she chose to write about the Bennett family, and in particular the trials and tribulations that Elizabeth and her sister Jane went through before finally catching two worthy husbands.

Your story has already been chosen, but now you need to look at it in the light of making it interesting and readable. Be ruthless, get rid of anything which does not fit in with your plot and story and concentrate on those parts which do.

Back story

Your story will also have to cover what has gone on before the start of the book – this is called the back story. In *Pride and Prejudice* the back story is that the family home is left to Mr Collins, a cousin of Jane and Elizabeth. It impinges on the plot when he decides to marry one of his cousins and is turned down by Elizabeth.

The importance of a back story and how to incorporate it is discussed later.

> **Top tip**
>
> One of the most important things to remember is that a story has a beginning, a middle and an end – but not necessarily in that order.

Quest

Whether there is only one, or seven or more universal storylines or plots, ultimately they are all about a quest of one kind or another: a journey to reach a goal. In *Pride and Prejudice* it is about finding a husband. Needless to say this journey is not a smooth one – otherwise there wouldn't be a book. In line with the dramatic arc the hero, or in this case heroine, has to overcome many obstacles, each one being more difficult than the one before.

Look at your life story and decide what your quest is, then what the obstacles are which have to be overcome before the resolution. The quest doesn't have to stay the same throughout the book, but any change should be as a result of a specific action not because it happens to suit.

Characters

It is common practice for novelists to base their characters on people they know or have observed. Sometimes they will make changes to the characters or combine characteristics from two or more people.

But you are starting with a group of people who already exist and have their own faults, foibles and virtues, so you will have to decide whether to:

- include everyone
- combine two or more to make the story easier to write or more dramatically satisfying
- add fictional characters to help progress the story.

The first criterion is to make the story readable. It should also follow the dramatic arc or basic shape of a conventional novel (see Chapter 14). If this means getting rid of some of your characters or combining them into one, then that is a route you should explore.

There is nothing wrong with adding a fictional character or two if:

- this helps to move your story forwards
- they add more obstacles to delay the final resolution
- they provide a foil to other characters (or all three).

Top tip

If you don't want people to recognize themselves, particularly if you are showing them in a bad light, then you will need to disguise them. This can be done by changing their sex, making them older or younger or putting them in a different setting or context.

Main character

The most common way to tell a story is to follow the fortunes of one main character – or protagonist as they are usually called when writing any form of drama. In *Pride and Prejudice* Elizabeth is the main character and we see the story from her point of view. As everyone is the hero of their own life, in your fictionalized life story, the main character is going to be you.

However, if your life story is just the starting point for the novel then you can choose any of your characters to be the protagonist.

Sometimes novels have two central characters, rather like the buddy movie format. They both need to be strong characters and it helps if they are opposites in some way. If you have a strong character in your life story you will need to decide whether they will become an equal protagonist with you and whether they will need to be re-written to provide conflict between the two of you (for more about conflict see later).

Other characters

To prevent your novel from becoming completely unwieldy you will have to decide which of your characters will be playing a major role in the story and which a minor. Darcy is a major character, as is Elizabeth's sister Jane, but the rest of the sisters are minor characters.

Major characters will need their own back story such as Darcy's relationship with Wickham. Minor characters will need less back story and are often only given certain characteristics to distinguish them. For example, Lydia is flirtatious and silly, Kitty is easily led and resentful and Mary is pious and pompous.

Setting

If you intend your novel to stick closely to you life story, you probably won't change the setting much, if at all. But if it is just a starting point for your novel you can set it anywhere and in any time.

Viewpoint

There are three viewpoints:

- first person
- third person
- detached narrator.

First person

As your novel is based on your life story then writing in the first person, with you as the protagonist, would seem an obvious choice. It makes the drama more intense and focussed. You are also able to control how much information you give the reader, and have the option to withhold information to create suspense.

Third person

Most novels are written in the third person, but still from the protagonist's point of view. However, like writing in the first person, the reader can only see things from the protagonist's point of view.

Detached narrator

This option is sometimes called the omniscient viewpoint because it allows the writer to move between the viewpoints of several characters.

Tense

As with writing traditional memoirs you have a choice of using:

- the past tense: which is the more common
- the present tense: which pulls the reader in and gives a sense of immediacy to your writing.

Don't worry if the above sounds prescriptive. The main thing is to write your story and then check that all the necessary components for a novel are in place and in the right order. If they aren't then make the necessary changes.

Exercise

Plan your life story as if it were a novel.

Describe the plot in one sentence.

List the main points of the story and the major characters.

Summary

In this chapter you have learnt:

- about the components of a novel
- about setting
- about viewpoints.

section four

getting published

16

conventional publishing

In this chapter you will learn:
- what publishers want
- how to find a publisher
- how to approach a publisher.

In matters of truth the fact that you don't want to publish something is, nine times out of ten, a proof that you ought to publish it.

Gilbert K. Chesterton

Having written your book, you may then want to try to get it published. The dream of most writers is for it to be snapped up by a well-known publisher, who will not only take on the task of printing and distribution, but will also pay royalties.

Generally speaking life stories which are snapped up are written by people who are:

- famous
- an expert in their field
- have achieved something momentous
- have been caught up in a current event
- have a track record as a writer.

In fact if you fall into these categories, publishers will probably have beaten a path to your door already.

But that doesn't mean that books about ordinary people don't get published – it just means you will have to put in some time and effort, and face rejection. It also has to be said there is an element of luck involved – your proposal could land on a publisher's desk just at the time they were thinking about including a life story like yours in their catalogue. But you can help to make your own luck by submitting to the right publishers and not giving up when faced with rejection.

What publishers want

The first thing they want is to make money. They can't afford to publish books which they don't think will appeal to the public and therefore won't sell. This doesn't mean they always get it right, there are many stories about publishers turning down bestsellers – *Harry Potter and the Philosopher's Stone* for example – until one finally takes a chance and then makes a killing.

To increase your chances of getting accepted you need to do your homework and then catch their attention. This is where the all important choice of a title and the opening paragraph comes in. If the title is bland, boring or meaningless the publisher may not even bother to look at the first page. And if your opening paragraph is boring, bland and predictable they probably won't read any further.

Finding a publisher

Not all publishers are interested in publishing memoirs so it is essential to do some research rather than wasting time and money sending submissions to the wrong ones.

A first step is to check who is publishing memoirs by looking to see who has published the ones on your bookshelves. If this doesn't give you enough information, go to the library and check through the books there.

> **Top tip**
> Look to see if a publisher specializes in certain types of memoirs or whether they publish all kinds.

Cross-reference these publishers with the lists of publishers in the *Artists' and Writers' Yearbook* or *The Writer's Handbook*. These books are published annually and you can either buy them or check them in the library. The information should tell you whether the publisher:

• will look at unsolicited manuscripts
• does not accept unsolicited manuscripts
• wants submissions through an agent.

Will look at unsolicited manuscripts

These are the publishers you will be sending your submission to so check their websites for further information. Look at their catalogue of titles which will tell you the types of life stories they have published and what percentage of their publications are life stories. If the percentage is low they may be less interested than publishers who have a high percentage.

It is also useful to see how recently the life stories were published. Publishing houses change their policies over time and one which published lot of life stories in the past may no longer be doing so.

No unsolicited manuscripts

If an entry says they do not accept unsolicited manuscripts it is still worthwhile sending an enquiry letter (see later).

Submissions through an agent

Publishers use agents to filter out the books which might be unsaleable. However, getting an agent is a chicken and egg situation – it is difficult to get an agent to take you on if you have no track record and it is difficult to get a track record if you do not have an agent. At this stage ignore publishers who want submissions via an agent.

> **Top tip**
>
> Don't neglect small publishing houses – they may be more willing to take you on than the large ones.

Make a list of potential publishers, concentrating on those which specialize in your type of life story. When making your choices don't forget to look at how long their books normally are. There is no point in submitting to a publisher who habitually publishes books of 100,000 words or more if your memoir is only 30,000.

> **Top tip**
>
> Calculate number of words in a published book by counting one page and multiplying by the number of pages. A rougher estimate of the number of words on a page can be calculated by counting the number of words in three paragraphs, averaging them and multiplying the number of paragraphs by that figure.

The approach

Now that you have a list of possible publishers, spend some more time on getting your approach right. This may be your only bite at the cherry so don't leave anything to chance.

Some publishers' websites state exactly what they require regarding submissions. It may be that they will even take them by email. Most, however, prefer to receive submissions by post – and nothing is guaranteed to get your submission dumped in the bin quicker than addressing it to Dear Sir or Madam. You have your list so ring each publisher up and ask for the name of the person that you should send your submission to.

Also ask for their correct title. Large publishing houses will have a separate commissioning editor for each genre i.e. thrillers, romance, autobiographies, while smaller ones may just have one commissioning editor. Finally ask if they want a full submission or an enquiry letter.

The submission

Publishers do not want a complete manuscript sent to them – they don't have time to read it. What they want is a submission which tells them about you, your life story and why it has reader appeal.

You should include:

- a covering letter
- a brief outline or synopsis of your life story
- sample chapters
- a CV if relevant
- cuttings of any articles which have been published
- a stamped addressed envelope.

Covering letter

This should include four things:

- **What** your life story is about: There is no need to go into too much detail because you will also be including an outline or synopsis, but try to capture the essence of it in a paragraph. And try to make that paragraph striking. Also add what genre it is and what its proposed length or number of words will be.
- **Who** you are: Tell them something about yourself – who you are and what you have done could be a deciding factor in whether you get accepted. For example if you are an expert in your field or have done something amazing. Again don't go into too much detail because if you have a lot to say that should go in your CV. It helps if you have had other books or articles published. It also helps if you can show how you are able to help publicize the book.

- **Why** you think your life story will appeal to readers: In other words you have got to sell your book to the publisher. If you know that there is already a large group of people who want to buy it, for example a history society or your regiment, then tell the publisher. In fact it is always useful to do some homework on likely markets.

- **How** it will fit with the publisher's other books: Make it clear that you have done your homework and understand the type of life stories they publish. If yours is similar to their others say it will fit in. If yours is different explain how it will enhance their catalogue.

> **Top tip**
> Put yourself in the publisher's shoes and think what you would want to know about a writer and their submission.

Example:

Dear

I see from your catalogue that you have published several sports-related autobiographies and wonder if you would be interested in mine.

It is entitled *From Nought to Ninety in Five Seconds*, subtitled *The memoirs of a Nonagenarian*, and is based on my life in the car racing industry. It gives an inside view of the thrills, spills and rivalries of Formula One from before the Second World War to the 1980s when I was lucky enough to observe at close quarters what really went on behind the scenes in those early days.

I have worked as an engineer on high-powered engines all my life and have always been fascinated by the magic of the combustion engine. In fact my earliest memories are of passing tools to my father as he tinkered with the family car.

I have worked with all the top racing car manufacturers and even after retirement have still kept in touch with many of the top drivers. I still go to watch Grand Prix racing and I was also lucky enough to take part in the Monte Carlo Rally in the 1970s.

I have already sold some articles based on my racing anecdotes to various magazines and several car clubs have expressed an interest in my book. Even though I am in my ninetieth year I am more than happy to help promote the book and give talks to interested groups.

I have enclosed two sample chapters, cuttings of the articles and my CV.

I look forward to hearing from you.

Yours sincerely

> **Top tip**
>
> Don't tell the publisher that your book is copyright: this indicates you are an amateur because all written work is automatically the copyright of the writer (see later and Chapter 04).

Approach your letter professionally, keep to the point and don't waffle. Try to keep to one page and don't try to make it funny, even if you are writing a humorous life story. Definitely avoid anything gimmicky to catch the commissioning editor's attention – it won't, it will be binned.

Brief outline or synopsis

Write a paragraph on each chapter. This is where the time you spent clarifying what kind of life story you wanted to write and getting the chapters right should pay dividends. Nothing is more off-putting to a publisher than a woolly description.

Sample chapters

Some publishers may want the first 5,000 words, others may want the first chapter, others may ask for two chapters. If they don't specify what they require, send the first chapter because this shows the publisher that you know how to hook the reader – it also sets up what to expect in the rest of the book. Then choose your best chapter to show that your standard of writing in the first chapter is maintained throughout.

> **Top tip**
>
> Don't staple the pages together, but do make certain they are numbered and have the title of your book as well as your name and a contact number at the bottom of each page, just in case they become separated from your letter.

CV

Your CV should list:

- any other books you have had published
- any articles relating to your memoirs which have been published, and where
- any other paid for writing
- any writing qualifications you have, for example in journalism or advertising
- any qualifications which are relevant to your memoirs.

There are some dos and don'ts for writing a good CV:

- Type it, don't handwrite it.
- Keep it to one page.
- Use white or cream paper with a simple font such as Ariel or Times New Roman.
- Start with your name, address, phone number, email address and mobile number.
- List your writing activities and successes (remembering to add to this with each new achievement).
- Don't waffle, keep it short, succinct and easily readable.
- Don't use fancy gimmicks or fancy layouts or photographs.
- Don't rely on a computer spellchecker, read it through carefully to check for errors.

Cuttings

These should only include copies of any articles you have had published in magazines – not letters to the letters page even if you were paid for them.

Top tip

When you remove a cutting from a publication always take the whole page, so that you include the header or footer where the name of the publication and the date are shown. Send photocopies, never the originals, as they probably won't be returned to you.

Stamped addressed envelope

There is some debate about whether you should include a stamped addressed envelope to have your sample chapters returned to you. If you send one then it is easy for the publisher to pop your submission in it and send it back – however there are no guarantees that they will have the time to do this, or that it won't get lost somewhere in the system.

On the other hand, including one shows a lack of belief in your book, and as it is unlikely you could re-use the sample chapters why ask for them back. If the publisher specifies that you should send one then do so, otherwise don't.

However, it is a good idea to include a stamped addressed postcard for the publisher to return so that you know your proposal has been received, although again there is no guarantee they will use it. Some publishers automatically acknowledge receipt and others don't.

Top tip
Make sure you include the correct amount of postage on your submission and your sae.

An enquiry letter will be virtually the same as the letter above, but you will only include your CV.

Multiple submissions

Should you send submissions to more than one publisher at a time? Publishers don't like this, but as it can sometimes take many weeks to receive a reply it could take years for you to work your way through your list.

At this stage all you are doing is submitting a proposal to see if they are interested, so if time is of the essence then it is reasonable to send out more than one submission at a time.

However, don't send an identical letter to each publisher. Not only should it be addressed by name to the correct person, you should also make it clear that you have done your homework regarding their catalogue.

Of course, if your memoirs are accepted then it is polite to contact the other publishers you have written to, to tell them.

If you find yourself in the happy position of more than one publisher wanting your book then this might be good time to find an agent to get you the best deal.

Reminders

If you have not heard from a publisher after six months then send a polite reminder about your proposal. Again, there is no guarantee you will get a reply. If you have heard nothing after a year then it is probably safe to assume you have been rejected.

Rejection

There is no getting round it – rejection is hurtful, particularly as this is your baby. But as said above, many top writers including J. K. Rowling of Harry Potter fame, have been rejected at some time in their career, so you are in good company.

If you are lucky, the publisher will tell you why you are being rejected, but most don't have the time. If you do get some feedback then take note of what they say, make the necessary changes and then either send your book back to them if you have been invited to, or find another publisher.

Not knowing why you have been rejected is more difficult. It could be that despite your hard work in trying to find the right publisher they decided not to publish any more life stories. Or they may already have a similar one waiting to be printed.

The main thing to remember is that *you* are not being rejected only your book and there are other ways of getting it published (see Chapters 18 and 19).

Finally, if a publisher responds positively, but asks you for money treat them with caution – they could be vanity publishers (see Chapter 18).

Summary

In this chapter you have learnt:

- how to write a submission
- how to write a CV
- what to do about rejection.

17

acceptance by a publisher

In this chapter you will learn:
- about publishing personnel
- about the publishing process
- about your responsibilities.

A poet can survive everything but a misprint.

Oscar Wilde

Acceptance by a bona fide publisher is a red letter day for any writer, so take the opportunity to have a well-deserved celebration. Then it's back down to earth and the realities of getting your manuscript up to scratch.

Publishing personnel

This is probably a good place to look at the people who will be taking charge of your book and what each does. Because some of them may well be freelancers there is sometimes a doubling up or overlapping of functions, but in the main they are:

- commissioning editor – sometimes called an acquisition editor
- peer reviewer
- editor – sometimes called a copy-editor or desk editor
- designer
- proofreader
- production editor
- marketing and sales executives.

Commissioning editor

This is the person who agreed to accept your book and with whom you will deal with most. Build a good relationship with them because they will be involved in every stage of the production of your book and will support you through the process of turning it into a saleable product.

They will organize your contract, sort out royalties and advances, and be responsible for ensuring you keep to deadlines.

Peer reviewer

If your life story contains specialist information, such as scientific, academic or sports-related material, some publishers might send the manuscript to a peer reviewer for their assessment before it is accepted by the commissioning editor.

Editor

It is their responsibility to go through your manuscript checking for spelling, grammar and consistency of style and voice.

If necessary they will give advice on structure, content and illustrations. They will also check for any libellous content and reach agreement with the writer to resolve any issues. Finally they will be responsible for 'marking up' the manuscript so that it can be typeset or formatted. This may also include choosing the typeface, design of chapter headings etc., but this is usually done by the designer.

Designer

They are responsible for the look of the book and will choose which typefaces will be used, what the chapter headings will look like and give advice on illustrations. But most importantly, they will design the front cover of the book which is often the reason why a book is picked up and bought.

Proofreader

Once the manuscript has been typeset, or these days formatted electronically, ready for printing, it is the job of the proofreader to check that the formatting is correct and that there are no typos (errors in formatting) such as a change in font size, bold or italicized print where there shouldn't be.

Production editor

They are responsible for the practical side of production and deal with typesetters, printers and bookbinders.

Marketing and sales executives

They will try to ensure your book is promoted and sold to all the major retailers – although it is worth bearing in mind that not all retailers take all books so you might not find yours sitting on the shelves in your local bookshop.

The publishing process

Before your book is accepted your proposal will have been read by a reader, possibly the peer reviewer, who will give an assessment on whether it is a viable proposition and whether it needs any alterations or additions such as moving chapters around or adding an extra one. Armed with this assessment, your commissioning editor will take the proposal to an editorial meeting with those involved in the production process, including the marketing and sales executives, who will decide whether it has saleability.

Contract

Once it has been agreed to accept your book your commissioning editor will issue you with a contract. If you are a member of the Society of Authors or the Writers' Guild of Great Britain they will vet the contract for you. Otherwise you will have to go through it yourself. Read every word so that you completely understand what you are signing, or ask your solicitor to look at it.

For instance, new technologies like 'print on demand', which allows short print runs, are causing changes to the standard clauses on minimum print levels and reversion rights (where the rights are returned to the author after their book has been out of print for a period of time). There are books which will help you, (see Appendices) and the *Writers' and Artists' Yearbook* usually has a section on what to look for in a contract.

Don't let your excitement at being accepted stop you from asking for changes in the contract if you feel that you are signing away your rights. If your requests are reasonable then the publisher will probably agree to them. If they are unwilling to make any alterations to the clauses then you will have to decide whether to accept the contract or decline the offer.

Royalties and advances

Royalties are the percentage of the book's cover price which is paid to the author. This can be between 7.5 and 10 per cent. Sometimes a publisher will pay the author an advance on the royalties. This might be paid when the proposal has been accepted or when the book has been completed. The author won't earn any more royalties until the publisher has earned the advance back from sales.

The media often runs stories of huge advances being paid to celebrities for their life stories, but this only happens if the publisher can be certain of a high volume of sales.

Deadlines

At some stage you will be given a deadline for the completion of your book. If it is already written this shouldn't prove a problem. If you haven't completed it then you will have to work out a timetable to ensure you can meet the deadline. While famous writers might get away with ignoring deadlines, you are unlikely to be so lucky and could find your contract terminated.

If circumstances arise which make it difficult or impossible to get it written by the agreed date, tell your commissioning editor straightaway so that the publisher can make the necessary adjustments to their schedules.

> **Top tip**
> Always allow more time than you think for checking your manuscript for errors before sending it off.

The editing process

If the editor feels that the structure of your book needs changing, such as the arrangement of your chapters, adding in more content or removing repetitious material, don't dismiss this advice out of hand.

While you may feel that your book is perfect already, remember these are professional people who know what sells and what doesn't. Remember also that the editor is not emotionally involved with your book in the same way you are, and that they are bringing an objective and dispassionate eye to your writing and will be able to pick up any flaws.

If you feel very strongly that you don't want to make any changes then you need to be able to back up your arguments – otherwise take their advice which is, after all, designed to improve your book.

Copy-editing

Once any structural alterations have been agreed the manuscript is thoroughly checked for spelling, grammar and consistency of style. At this stage there may be some minor re-writing.

Formatting

The manuscript is then formatted by the editor ready for typesetting.

Proofreading

Once the manuscript is formatted a few copies will be printed off for proofreading. This is done by both a proofreader and the author and this will probably be the first time you will get an idea of what the finished book will look like. It won't have its cover but it will look like a book.

If the publishers include more than one proofreading stage, you will be able to make alterations to the text during the first stage, but at the final proofreading stage you will only be able to check for spelling, grammatical errors or any formatting abnormalities such as bold lettering where it shouldn't be. If you insist on making any alterations during the final proofreading you may have to pay for them.

Extras

During the editing process other members of the editorial staff will assign your book its International Standard Book Number (ISBN), write the information which will go on the back cover and possibly organize your photo, as the author.

Details of the book, including the publication date, will already have been circulated to the bookshops and Internet companies such as Amazon.com. Finally the book will be printed and bound.

Rights

You own the copyright of everything that you write, and when you sell your story to a publisher you are actually selling them the right to use your words in book form. The publisher will then own the rights to your book, although some authors do retain their copyright. If you are hoping for worldwide sales it is a good idea to get professional advice on selling your rights.

Electronic rights

These are the right to publish books in a digital form on the Internet, CD-ROMS, disks etc. and as the writer you own these rights until you sell them to someone else. Because of new technologies coming along this is a constantly changing field, and legislation concerning electronic rights – and the publishers' approach to them – is also changing rapidly. If you sign a contract selling your First British Serial Rights (FBSR) or your First American Serial Rights (FASR) check to see if any electronic rights have been included and whether you are happy with the contract's conditions.

Again if you are a member of the Society of Authors they may be able to help you find your way through the wording.

Because ownership of electronic rights is a comparatively new area, and has been the subject of several court cases, the legalities of ownership are outside the remit of this book.

Marketing

Although the publishers will have a marketing strategy and will send out review copies to national papers and any relevant magazines, you will probably be asked how you can help with publicity and sales as well.

Press releases

To help sell more copies of your book it is worthwhile sending your own press releases to your local papers and radio stations in the hope of getting a write-up. Follow the same advice as for finding a publisher i.e. ring the newspaper or radio station and find out who it should be sent to. As most press releases are now sent by email, get an email address.

Finding an angle

The first thing to remember is that the media isn't interested in helping you sell books – you can pay for an advert to do that – what reporters want are interesting news stories and photo opportunities. So you will need to select either something of special interest from the book or something of special interest about yourself which makes a good story. Just being a local writer may not be enough.

From the book

Does it contain a personal perspective of a well-known person or event? Does it describe how you managed to get back stage at the Beatles' first concert or meet the Queen? If you have always lived in the area does your life story feature well-known local people and places long gone?

About you

This is no time to be a shrinking violet so if you have any claim to fame now is the time to use it. If you have been a member of parliament, a county councillor, GP or chairman of the local Ramblers Association this could be the hook to get the media interested in your book.

If you are extremely young or getting on in years, that could be newsworthy – for example 'ten-year-old writes memoirs' or 'octogenarian publishes first book'.

Photo opportunity

Try to persuade your local bookshop to not only stock your book, but also organize a book signing day. Then send a press release and also ask for a press photographer to come along. Just in case the press don't send anyone, get someone to take a photo for you to send to the paper along with all the details about the book.

Writing a press release

Having decided on your angle, you will need an eye-catching headline. Although this may not be used in the paper – sub editors prefer to put their own headlines on stories – this is the first thing the news editor will read so it has to be catchy. Follow the same rules for choosing a book title and remember to keep it short.

Your opening paragraph should explain your title in an intriguing way to hook the news editor in and subsequent paragraphs should expand on the angle.

In the excitement of writing don't forget to include the relevant information about your book, including its title, the name of the publisher, where it is available and the price.

Use a common font such as Times New Roman size 12 and double space the text. Write 'press release' in capitals at the top and centre it. Underneath put the headline in normal case but bold. After the last paragraph write 'End'. Under that write your contact details, including your name, phone number and email address. If you can provide a picture then say so.

Example:

PRESS RELEASE

A fishy tale

An octogenarian, who has just published his first book, will be signing copies of his memoirs in the Book Boutique, Meadow Street, Anytown, on Monday, 21 August from 10 a.m. In it, John Smith, who held his first fishing rod at the age of two, reminisces about his greatest catches, both here and in Canada.

Entitled *The ones that didn't get away*, John takes the reader through his idyllic childhood spent fishing for tiddlers from the river bank near his home in Anytown to catching salmon in Alaska. He even managed to find time to cast a line during the final days of World War II when as a young private he found himself in France.

Although he has now turned 85 John has no intention of packing away his canvas stool and keep net, in fact he is planning to enter next month's angling competition.

The book, which has been published by Anytown Publications, normally sells for £9.99, but at the book signing they will be sold at a special 20 per cent discount.

END

For the attention of the news editor.

Could a press photographer be sent to cover the book signing? If not I can provide a photo.

Contact details:

John Smith

Address

Telephone number

Email address

If you have provided enough information in the press release then it may just be given a slight re-write to conform to the paper's house style and then used, otherwise a reporter will contact you for more information or perhaps to find another angle.

If the paper doesn't want an email – and most do because it saves time inputting it on their computer – post it or fax it.

If your local radio station shows an interest then go on air and plug your book. Although you are reliant on the interviewer's questions don't forget to get in all the details about it.

Coping with criticism

Finally, should your book be snapped up then you need to be aware that it could be publicly criticized. If the criticism is valid, take it on the chin, if possible do the necessary re-writes or don't make that mistake again in your second book. If it is not valid ignore it. And remember, it is all too easy to criticize someone else's work and a lot harder to actually write something. At least you have written a book which has been published – so be proud of that.

Summary

In this chapter you have learnt:

- what a commissioning editor does
- about electronic rights
- how to cope with criticism.

18
self publishing

In this chapter you will learn:
- about full self publishing
- about partial self publishing
- how to market your book.

For many, self publishing may be the only way of getting a book published and made available to a wider audience. Self publishing an attractive book can enhance the life writing experience – resulting in a cherished memento or a book available for sale.

Jane Rowland, Editor of *The Self Publishing Magazine*

Literally speaking, self publishing means that you become the publisher and pay all the people needed to produce your book, such as editors, printers, designers and bookbinders.

It was stigmatized for many years, particularly when vanity publishing was shown to be costing would-be-authors thousands of pounds to get their books into print. It was also felt in some quarters that if an author wasn't good enough to get a proper publisher to take their book on then it was down right foolish or self indulgent to pay to have it printed.

This is not the case in the USA where self publishing is considered an acceptable way of getting your book into print. Attitudes are also starting to change in the UK.

Of course, self publishing is not a new phenomenon: many well-know authors including Charles Dickens, Charlotte Brontë, Virginia Woolf, Mark Twain and Jane Austen were all happy to pay to have their books published to begin with.

More recently best-selling authors Graham Taylor, who wrote *Shadowmancer,* Christopher Paolini who wrote *Eragon* (made into a film in 2006), and life story writers Stephen Clarke who wrote *A Year in the Merde* and Shally Hunt of *The Sea on our Left* fame, self published before being snapped up by conventional publishers.

Considering self publishing

While self publishing is not a guaranteed route to fame and fortune it is an option worth considering if:

- you only want copies for family and friends
- you are happy to pay to have something concrete to show for all your hard work
- you feel you don't have time to wait for conventional publishers to make up their minds
- you have a guaranteed market where you can recoup your outlay
- you have an unshakeable faith in your book.

However, do bear in mind that if you are hoping to attract the attention of a conventional publisher then you must be prepared to put a lot of effort into publicity and marketing to build up substantial sales.

Subscriptions

Even if you hope to recoup your costs from sales you will still have to pay up front for any services you use. One way of raising money to pay for your book is to seek subscriptions from interested readers. If your life story is going to appeal to a particular group, for example members of club or society, they may be willing to subscribe towards the cost of getting it printed.

It will depend on what arrangement you have with your subscribers whether they get a free copy or not. However, you might want to list them in the prelim pages, unless specifically asked not to, as a way of saying thank you.

There are two options for self publishing:

• full
• partial.

Full self publishing

If you choose this option you will need to find all the tradesmen yourself, such as editors, printers and bookbinders. This will give you complete control over all aspects of publishing your book and all the profits from its sale. However you will be responsible for every part of the publishing process and if you want to make a profit you will need to spend time and effort getting the best deals.

While it pays to shop around to get the best prices, it also pays to try to use local tradesmen with whom you can build a relationship. You will find most of these in the *Yellow Pages* under publishing services.

Choosing a name

As you are now going to be a publisher – even if this is going to be your only book – why not give yourself a proper name such as: A.J.G. Publishing or Ashmead Press. By separating the publisher's name from the author's name your book will look less like a self published one – which may be useful should you decide to use wholesalers or distributors (see later).

Associations

As a publisher it may also pay you to join the IPG (Independent Publishers Guild) a UK organization that looks after smaller and independent publishers – their website is **www.ipg.uk.com** and has some useful tips and information on it. Many self publishers have joined them – even if they've only got one book – as this allows them to network with other IPG members and take discounted space at book fairs on the IPG stand etc. (see later).

There are similar organizations in the USA. The Small Publishers Association of North America **www.spannet.org/** offers help and advice on production, distribution, shipping and marketing as well the opportunity to network.

Having set yourself up as a bona fide publisher it is now time to get your manuscript up to scratch for publishing. There are several steps which have to be taken before you can finally hold your book in your hand.

Editorial tasks

Editing

Unless you are completely sure of your ability to look at your work objectively – and make the necessary changes – it is well worth paying someone else to edit it. As the writer we are often too close to our work and find it difficult to see the wood for the trees. We also find it hard to cut out what we believe to be our best bits, but a good editor will home in on patches of purple prose and edit them out.

Proofreading

No matter how many times a manuscript is proofread some errors will still slip through. You can cut down on this by persuading someone else to read it as well, as they may pick up on the ones that you have missed.

> **Top tip**
>
> If you can persuade them, you can use friends or family members for this, preferably more than one.

Design

This covers both the cover and the inside of your book. Unless you have some knowledge or expertise in this area, one of the best ways of picking up ideas is to look at books which have been professionally published. This time, rather than reading them, analyze what makes them look good.

Covers

Whether we like it or not, readers do judge a book by its cover so it is worthwhile giving some thought on how to make yours stand out. Look at the best-sellers and analyze what makes their covers work. Are their titles easy to read? Is the design simple or complicated? Does it tell you anything about the book?

If you have a flair for design or know someone who could draw a memorable cover for you then that will be a saving. But if you can't be sure of coming up with something eye-catching it might better to spend some money on getting a professional designer to do it for you.

> **Top tip**
>
> Don't forget you will also have to decide what to put on the back cover and the spine, which is sometimes the first part of the book a potential buyer sees when browsing along the bookshop shelves.

Inside

Inside is equally important. It is up to you to decide which typeface and font size you want, what your chapter headings will look like and whether you want paragraphs indented or given a space in between.

Don't make the print too small so that it is difficult to read or too large so that it looks like a toddler's book. On an aesthetic level, the width of margins and gutters could show the difference between a professional or amateur design. Again if you are not sure it might be better to get a professional designer to do it.

Size and quality

Books come in all shapes and sizes and it is important to pick a size which will best enhance your book. Your choice could depend on the number of words you have written and the number of illustrations and photos you plan to include. A 100,000-word book packed with photos may not look its best if it is crammed into an A5 or paperback size.

You will also have to choose what kind of paper you want it printed on. Paper comes in two types: coated, which is what glossy magazines use, and uncoated which is what is generally used in books. It also comes in various thicknesses which are measured by the number of grams it weighs per square metre. Most papers range between 80 and 130 grams and most paperback pages are printed on 80 gram paper.

Illustrations

If you are including photos or other forms of illustration you will need to decide the best way to use them. Will you have them on a page on their own or will you run the text around them? Will they be all together in the middle of the book or spread throughout? Will they be on glossy paper or on the same paper as the rest of the book?

Production necessities

ISBN

This stands for International Standard Book Number, a unique identifying number which is used to catalogue your book and enable bookshops to stock and order your book easily.

You don't have to have an ISBN if you are only selling or giving away your books to friends and family. However, if you want to sell your book commercially then you, as the publisher, will have to register and apply for a prefix number.

The ISBN has to be printed on the reverse side of the title page.

It also goes on the back cover, but before doing that you will need to convert it into a bar code.

The UK ISBN Agency is run by a company called Nielsen Book and they can be contacted on:

Tel: +44 (0) 870 777 8712

Email: **isbn.agency@nielsen.com**

Website: **www.isbn.nielsenbookdata.co.uk**

At the time of writing it costs £105.75 to register as a publisher. This will give you a publisher's prefix and ten ISBNs – they are only allocated in blocks of ten. They can either be emailed or posted to you.

For information about turning your ISBN into a bar code go to the Book Industry Communication website, **www.bic.org.uk**, click on 'ISBNs and bar codes', then on 'Barcoding' for books.

The US Agency for creating prefixes and ISBNs is R.R. Bowker, LLC, and they can be contacted on:

Toll Free/United States: 877–310–7333. All others: (+1) (908) 219–0273.

E-mail: **isbn-san@bowker.com**

Or via their ISBN website: **www.isbn.org**

At the time of writing it cost a minimum of $125. You can also order bar codes on the same form for an additional $25. This site also give links to other useful Bowker services and has advice for self publishers.

To find the agencies handling ISBNs in other countries go to the International ISBN Agency **www.isbn-international.org**.

Databases

If you want to market your book through wholesalers or distributors you will also need to get your title on one of the databases, such as Nielsen Book. As a new publisher, when you apply to Nielsen Book for your prefix and ISBNs you will receive an information pack which includes a 'new title form' asking for information about your book such as title, publication date, price, availability etc. This information is automatically added to the Nielsen Book database free of charge. However, you will need to complete a 'new title form' for every subsequent title you publish. The forms should be sent to Nielsen Book, 89–95 Queensway, Stevenage, Hertfordshire, SG1 1EA, so that they can add the information to their database.

For a fee, you can add even more information about your book (see their website).

> **Top tip**
> Fill in as much information as possible because this will help sell your book.

If you are going to distribute copies of your book to customers yourself any orders received for your book will be routed through to you by Nielsen Book's TeleOrdering service. If you are planning to use wholesalers or distributors (see later) then Nielsen will route the orders to them to handle.

There is plenty of useful information on the Nielsen BookData marketing website, their service for new publishers. There is also a very good help desk, click on 'contact us'.

The Nielsen Book database lists information for all English Language books, free of charge, no matter where they are published. See the Nielsen Book website **www.nielsenbook. co.uk.**

In the USA Bowker offers a similar services, see their website, **www.bowkerlink.com.**

Legal deposits

Publishers have to send a copy of their book to the British Library within one month of publication. The other five libraries which have to be sent copies are:

- The Bodleian Library, Oxford
- The University Library, Cambridge
- The National Library of Scotland, Edinburgh
- The Library of Trinity College, Dublin
- The National Library of Wales, Aberystwyth.

Printing

The advent of new digital technology in the 1990s, revolutionized the publishing industry, making it more cost-effective to go down the self publishing route.

Previously, the higher set-up costs of using conventional offset lithographic printing presses meant one or two thousand copies had to be printed off at a time to make it economic. Now it is viable to print off a few copies of a book using digital printing (similar to photocopying), as and when they are needed.

Many writers choose the digital printing method – however, if you believe that you will be able to sell hundreds of books then choose offset lithographic printing, because although it is more expensive to start with, on long runs it works out cheaper per book. But you will probably need to order one or two thousand at a time, all of which have to be stored and then sold.

Formatting

To get your book printed you have to get the manuscript from your computer to the printing company. This means formatting or typesetting it into a print-ready file, which can then be sent to them on a disk or by email.

Most writers use Microsoft Word programmes which only allow limited formatting. Also not all printing companies have the technology to accept Word files. If this is the case you either have to convert your manuscript to a PDF (portable document file) or format it using specialist software such as QuarkXpress, Adobe InDesign or Adobe PageMaker. So ask your printing company what form they can accept your manuscript in. If this is a one-off book it might be cheaper to pay someone to format it for you rather than buying a special software programme to do it yourself.

Top tip
You will get a more professional finish if your book is formatted using specialist software.

As in so many fields, printing technology is changing almost week by week and by the time you are reading this it could well have moved on again.

Bookbinding

Once your book has been printed it will have to be bound to hold it together. Most paperback books are bound by a process called Perfect Binding where the cover is glued to the spine.

Hardback books are Case Bound and the pages are stitched together in bundles.

Bookbinders can be found in trade directories or your printing company may be able to put you in touch with one.

Pricing

There is a top price for any book and if you go beyond that it will probably mean your book won't sell. Look at the prices of books similar to yours and use them as a guide. It is essential that the production costs of your book are low enough to give you a profit after everything has been paid for. Don't forget to add into your calculations the cost of posting books to customers or delivering them to bookshops as well as advertising and other promotional aids such as flyers and websites.

If you use a wholesale or distribution company (see later) you will also have to factor that cost in as well, because they will want a percentage of the cover price.

> **Top tip**
> Don't spend more on self publishing than you can afford to lose.

Marketing

Now that your book has been printed you will need to spend time and effort on selling it.

Friends and family

Getting your book published is an exciting event so celebrate with a book launch. A party is also a good way of thanking all those who have helped you get your life story into print. Make sure you have plenty of copies available for sale.

> **Top tip**
> Don't sell every copy at the party – you will need at least one to show latecomers. Take names and addresses instead and post copies later.

Wholesalers and distributors

Wholesalers buy in bulk from publishers and then sell the books on to the bookstores. This is advantageous to the bookstores because they only have to buy from one company rather than dozens of individual publishers.

The two main UK wholesalers are Gardners, www.gardners.com/gardners and Bertrams, www.bertrams.com/BertWeb. In the USA one of the largest is Ingram International www.ingraminternational.com.

Wholesalers will also buy books in small quantities – Gardners and Bertrams would probably initially order between one and ten copies from self publishers who have not yet built up a history of sales with them. But you will usually have to open an account with them before they can supply your book in bulk (which simply means filling in a form).

Before you contact a wholesaler you will need to make sure your book information is entered on to Nielson BookData as they are unlikely to order any title whose info is not on it (especially if it is from a unknown publisher). Finally, send your AI (Advance Information sheet) to the buyers at the wholesalers to give them the heads up about your title in advance of its publication.

Distributors are used by publishers to take on the tasks of invoicing, order fulfilment and returns – which can be a time-consuming process – as well as providing warehousing to store the books.

One of the largest of these is Littlehampton Books Services www.lbsltd.co.uk.

Book Web www.bookweb.co.uk/distributors has a list of distributors and also offers advice on how to choose a distributor. Or try www.esources.co.uk, click on 'suppliers', then 'publishing and printing', then 'books' for a list of smaller distributors.

Distributors, who are also members of the IPG may also be happy to represent other IPG members even if they have only one title. Check on the IPG for a list of members and their websites.

For a list of distributors in the USA try the Ingram Book Group website www.ingrambook.com, click on 'new to Ingram', then on 'publishers' in the menu. There you will find a list of distributors who take self published books.

You will be expected to pay for the distribution services as a percentage of the cover price on any books sold. You will also have to pay the distribution company to store your books – this can be charged per book or per pallet of books and is either per day or per month. Finally you will have to make sure your stock is insured – sometimes you have to organize the insurance and sometimes they do it for you.

There are pros and cons to using these specialist companies: you will have to sign up to terms and conditions if using distribution services, so read the small print as it could affect your profits. If it leads to increased sales then it is worthwhile, but the downside is they are costly and you could end up out of pocket and with a number of unsold books on your hands which have been hanging about in a warehouse.

This is a complex subject, but there is a very helpful article on *The Self Publishing Magazine* website: go to **www.selfpublishingmagazine.co.uk** and click on 'article library' where you can find the article on wholesalers as well as other articles on similar topics that may also be of interest.

In the UK, major book chains are still reluctant to take books unless they have come from a wholesaler, but even if you decide not to go down that route there are still opportunities to get your book into shops:

- Contact your local branch of a major chain because they may stock local authors.
- Try to persuade independent shops to take them – probably on a sale or return basis. Don't forget to offer to do book signings.
- Be innovative and ask your local newsagent, Post Office, butcher, greengrocer etc. to stock them.

Libraries

Many self publishers find most sales are to the library market. Libraries buy from distributors such as those mentioned above.

Having your books in libraries can also bring in an annual sum provided it is registered for Public Lending Rights. The payment is based on loans data collected from a sample of libraries. It is free to register books, but they will need an ISBN.

Contact PLR at: Richard House, Sorbonne Close, Stockton-on-Tees, TS17 6DA. Tel: +44 (0) 01642 604699, or check their website **www.plr.uk.com** for more information.

Online

A lot of books are now bought online so you will need to get yours listed. The sites most people turn to first are **www.amazon.co.uk** in the UK and **www.amazon.com** in the USA. Click on the relevant website then click on 'join advantage' (at the bottom of the web page) to see how you upload your details. Once a buyer requests your book Amazon will contact you so that you can post one off.

Websites

If you don't already have a website then it is essential to get one now so that you can put your book details on it. Include a couple of chapters so that readers can get a flavour of what it's about – then make certain you include all the details of how they can buy it.

Book fairs

If you have confidence in your book then taking it to book fairs could pay off. One of the largest is The London Book Fair **www.londonbookfair.co.uk/**. Other UK fairs are listed on the Writers Services website, **www.writersservices.com/ws_internat_bookfairs.htm**. At the time of writing this had not been updated recently but it is still worthwhile checking the websites listed for current information. For a list of book fairs in the USA, check out **www.loc.gov/loc/cfbook/bookfair.html**.

Be warned, however, that hiring a stand is an expensive business – unless you are a member of the IPG. You will also need to provide plenty of promotional material such as flyers for potential buyers to take away.

Press releases

Without a publisher's marketing machinery behind you, you will have to be both proactive and creative to generate publicity in the press. You will need to send out dozens of press releases and review copies to both the local and national media.

It is also time to think laterally:

- If your life story includes an element of travel then send press releases and review copies to travel magazines.
- If you include the time you spent in the armed services send them to the relevant associations.
- If you have included a lot about gardening then send them to gardening magazines.

- If you were a cook or housekeeper then send them to women and home magazines.
- If you have written a lot about your sports or hobbies then send them to the relevant sports or hobby magazines.
- If you have written a pet biography sent them to the relevant horse, dog, cat etc. magazines.
- If you have included a large section on your family tree send them to family research magazines.

Working with others

One way of sharing the load, and the cost of publishing books, is to get together with other writers. This is what Anne Brooke and a group of writers in Surrey have done.

Case study

Goldenford Publishers: four Surrey writers are doing it for themselves...

In 2004, we decided to set up our own publishing company, Goldenford Publishers (**http://www.goldenford.co.uk**), partly as we realized that commercial publishers were no longer accepting either good quality novels which were off-genre or those that they couldn't see 'where to place on the shelf' and also because Esme Ashford, a founder member of Guildford Writers and talented short story writer, had died the previous year and we wished to publish a collection of her work to commemorate her talent. So Esme's *On the Edge* was our first publication.

It sold very well locally and encouraged us to continue the venture and publish a book each. The money raised from the sales of each book partly finances the production of the next, and we take royalties from sales in the usual way. Recently we have been successful enough to hire a part-time marketing manager who is helping to raise awareness of Goldenford and as a result we have even been asked to speak at events abroad.

We found it was relatively easy to print books on demand to a very high standard through our printer, Antony Rowe, and their link with book distributors, Gardners, meant that sending books out to customers was also fairly simple. The very steep mountain we had to climb was of course marketing and letting people know the books were there. After much trial and error, we found that the best way of selling books was to arrange a big launch party and start the book's sales life with a flourish. After that, success came through organizing events and readings, arranging radio interviews, sending out regular press releases, attending farmers' markets and local shows, and attempting to have a reasonable relationship with local bookshops.

Still the fact remains that most of our sales come from direct contact with buyers at events and through personal recommendation and web marketing.

In conclusion, we can highly recommend setting up your own publishing company to writers who would like to take total control of the publishing process and begin to develop their own readership. It's surprisingly fun and immensely satisfying!

Anne Brooke

Partial self publishing

If you don't want to take on the work of finding all the tradesmen, particularly if you only want a few copies printed, the next best option is to use one of the specialist companies, which are basically service providers. In other words they find all the tradesmen to carry out each stage of the book's publication and will take your manuscript from you and turn it into a fully-fledged book.

You don't have to use all their services, and the more you can do yourself in the way of editing, proofreading and formatting, the less you will have to pay. However, you will still be the publisher and you will still own the copyright to your book.

Finding a specialist company

You don't have to surf far on the Internet to find dozens of companies offering to take your manuscript and turn it into a printed book. They can also be found in specialist self publishing magazines or writing magazines. Some sound too good to be true, and possibly are, so it pays to shop around and read the small print. What looks like a bargain may end up having hidden costs.

You can't beat a personal recommendation so if you know of anyone who has self published ask who they used and whether they were satisfied with the service.

If you don't know anyone, go to the library and look at life stories or other books which you think may have been self published to see who published them. This at least tells you the book was successfully self published and is in the shops or library. Then check the website of these publishers to see what they are offering.

You can always check on the quality of the books they print by ordering a copy of one of their latest titles, preferably from a major store or from Amazon.com. Although it means spending a bit of money, it could save you even more money in the long run if you are not satisfied with the product. Also by ordering from a bookshop or online, you are testing whether they are genuine when they say that they will get your book into all the major shops and online stores.

Top tip

Look out for articles in the local paper on writers who have recently had something published. If the book is of local interest, a volume of short stories or a book of their poems, then it is quite likely to have been self published so try to get in touch with them to ask about their experiences.

Each company will probably have a different package to offer so you need to know exactly what you want to do with your books. If it is your intention to have a few copies printed to give away or sell to a few friends and family then choose a package which allows a very short print run even though each book may be more costly. If you want to sell copies on a commercial basis then choose a package where the cost of the book is lower, but you will have to order more.

Points to look out for when assessing a specialist company

As both the author and the publisher, all rights to the content of the book, including electronic rights, should remain with you. This is essential because if a conventional publisher becomes interested you need to own the copyright otherwise you won't benefit from the royalties.

If you have provided the design for the cover, the rights to this should also remain with you, or if it has been provided by a professional designer, with them.

- Ensure that your copyright is shown on the reverse side of the title page.
- Get a quote for all the costs including shipping and printing illustrations both black and white and coloured.
- Check how much extra copies will cost to print.
- Check how easy it is to order more copies and how long they take to print.
- Check what weight and quality of paper will be used, both in the book and for the cover.
- Will it be acid-free?
- Check how the books will be bound:
  - saddle stitched – using staples
  - wire coil binding
  - perfect binding – more expensive but this is how most paperback books are bound
  - case binding – used for hardback books.
- Ensure there is a money-back guarantee if you are not happy with the quality of your book.
- Check if the company supplies the ISBN or whether you have to register yourself and obtain it.
- Check if they will deposit six copies with the legal deposit libraries or whether you have to. If they say they will do it you can check that they comply with this requirement by asking them for other titles they have printed and then checking that these have been deposited.
- Clarify how much publicity and marketing they do. If they say your book will be available in major bookstores and online, make sure you check that their other titles are available in major stores and online.

Presentation of manuscript

To keep costs down, it pays to present your manuscript edited, proofread and formatted to the publisher's requirements. If they have to do any of these they will charge for it. The good sites itemize exactly what extra services they offer and what each one will cost.

Vanity publishers

Vanity publishers, as opposed to genuine self publishing companies, take advantage of a writer's desire to see their book in print. Unfortunately they usually charge a lot of money to do it and the end product may be of poor quality.

Avoid them by following the advice given above and comparing the prices of several different service providers. At the time of writing, prices for having your book published can range from several hundred to several thousand pounds depending on the package on offer and how much work needs to be done on your manuscript.

> **Top tip**
> Steer clear of companies which offer subsidized publishing, they may then own the copyright to your book.

The secret is to take sensible precautions and only spend what you can afford, or can recoup from known sales. Don't be persuaded into spending way more than you can afford by a company telling you that your royalties will soon pay for the costs – they won't. Life stories, unless they are truly exceptional, don't sell in large numbers.

On the other hand, don't let anyone put you off self publishing. You have written a book and you have every right to see it in print.

Retired West-Country reporter Mary Frances decided she couldn't wait any longer for conventional publishers to take her book on so decided to give self publishing a go.

> **Case study**
> For as long as I can remember I have been writing something-or-other. Stories, books, plays and poems have littered my childhood, adolescence and grown-up-hood to the present day. From time to time I have submitted books to publishers and agents, but after spending what seemed like years in time, and a frightening number of pounds in postage, I usually gave up after the first two rejections and (on the principle of buying a new car when the ashtray is full), simply sat down and wrote another book.

Finally, however, after qualifying as a journalist at the age of 70, and after seven colourful years writing for other people in the local newspaper, I decided the time had come to retire and write solely for *me*! So I rounded up my old manuscripts, wrote another novel and polished up an autobiography – then looked round, yet again, for a publisher.

To my chagrin, I found that the problem had grown worse instead of better. Too many people must be writing books, I decided. So, adding up the possible months/years spent approaching publishers or agents, posting the required 50 pages and waiting more weeks/months each time for the verdict before starting the whole process again, I decided sadly that for a 77-year-old this was not a workable proposition. I simply didn't have enough years ahead.

Then my ex-husband told me of an advert in *Saga Magazine* for a publisher who, he thought, may be right for me. These offered neither classic self publishing where one pays printing costs, orders a minimum quantity and is then left with the job of selling the result, nor the traditional publishing method of waiting for the right person to spot one's talent and offer one a contract.

This publisher would produce my book for a standard charge, ranging from £500 plus to £1,000 plus, print it digitally only as ordered (so no print runs and no pile-up of copies in the garage) and then handle the retailing – mainly via the Internet and through my own webpage, but also, according to my choice of option, through the major shops and outlets. The copyright would remain mine, available to other publishers. All that was required was some computer know-how in order to format the book myself. Since I knew that whatever I couldn't do there were computer wizarding friends who could, and since the royalty offered was considerably higher than one expects from traditional publishers, I punched the air, said 'Yes', and signed the contract.

My first baby – the autobiography *The Song of the Spinning Sun* – was launched in November 2007. I now await my first royalty cheque. As well as Internet sales, more than 200 copies have been sold either by me personally or through word of mouth, so I am definitely into profit! And since there is a 15 per cent discount on second books, my next magnum opus, a humorous genre novel called *Alice McGinty's Goat*, the first in a (hopefully long) series, comes out in June 2008.

Mary Frances

Provided you go into self publishing with your eyes wide open there is no reason why you too shouldn't end up with a book to be proud of.

Summary

In this chapter you a have learnt:

- about printing
- about legal deposits
- what to look for in a specialist company.

19

publishing from home

In this chapter you will learn:
- how to produce a book at home
- how to print a book on your computer
- how to secure the pages.

The future belongs to those who believe in the beauty of their dreams.

Eleanor Roosevelt

If all you want to do is to print off a few copies for family and friends then this can be done with your home computer and printer. With a bit of time and care it is possible to produce an attractive, illustrated book with stiff covers like a paperback.

There are several ways of producing a book:

- A5 stapled booklet
- A4 stapled booklet
- A4 or A5 comb bound book
- A4 or A5 thermal bound book
- A4 or A5 in ring binder.

A5 stapled booklet

Although this looks like a proper book the disadvantages are:

This format can only be used for up to 100 pages of text because staplers can only cope with 25 sheets of paper.

You will need a specialist stapler.

The staples may rust after a while.

A4 80 gms is probably the best weight paper to use, and because the pages will have to be folded it is better to incorporate photographs and illustrations with the text rather than printing them separately on glossy paper.

Top tip

Because the quality and stiffness of 80 gram paper varies, test your paper by printing on both sides with both text and photos to check that the printing doesn't show through.

Formatting

The process may look complicated but taken step by step it is really quite simple.

First, prepare your text:

1 Incorporate your photos and illustrations into the text with their captions. If there is space and your skills are up to it,

use the wrap-around method to run text around the pictures.

2 If your text is in separate chapters put all the chapters into one document. Put page breaks between each chapter so that each one starts on a new page.

3 Because you are limited to the number of pages, decide which of the extras to include at the beginning and the end. It is up to you whether you decide to put in a dedication or a list of chapters and photographs or a foreword – you don't have to. When you have chosen the extras, slot them into the relevant part of the main document and put page breaks between them.

4 Click on 'file' and in the menu go to 'page set-up' and put the document into A5 portrait. Change the margins to 1 cm top and bottom and both sides to give more space on each page for text.

5 Change text to a clear, reasonable size font: 11 or 12 point Times New Roman works well.

6 Justify your text on both sides by clicking on the relevant icon on the tool bar. Documents are usually justified on the left side only, but to create the look of a book it is necessary for both sides to be justified.

7 Check to see that the title, dedications or any other extras are in the correct positions on their pages. Check that photos and captions are next to each other. Also check to see that there are no orphans and widows.

Orphans are when the first line of a paragraph appears at the bottom of one page and the rest of the paragraph appears on the next. Click on return until the first line moves across to the second page.

Widows are similar but are when the last part of paragraph appears on the second page. This is more difficult to adjust as moving the rest of the paragraph to the second page could leave quite a gap at the bottom of the first page. There are three ways of resolving this:

- If it is only a few words try to reduce the length of the paragraph by re-writing it so that it all fits on the first page.
- If there are only two or three lines on the first page put an extra gap between the other paragraphs on that page until you have moved the whole paragraph to the second page.
- Split the paragraph into two separate paragraphs so that there is one on each page.

Top tip

If you reduce the document down to 50 per cent size you will be able to see three pages at a time, which makes it easier to make adjustments.

8 Save this document.

9 Make a note of how many pages long the document is. When you come to make up the dummy book (see later) you will need to divide the number of pages by four – if necessary rounding the figure up. This is because there will be four pages printed on each A4 sheet, two on each side. For example if your document has 27 pages you will need to use seven pages of A4 to create your book – the last page being blank.

Next, you are going to create a series of files that you will print from. Each file will hold two pages of the finished book.

10 Using scrap paper, take the number of sheets required and make a dummy book, numbering the pages – this will act as a template for working out which pages have to go together for printing purposes. You may wish to number extra prelim pages differently from the main text pages.

11 On the computer create a new A4 file. Go into 'page set-up' and make the margins the same as the main document and change setting from portrait to landscape.

12 Open the file and insert two columns. Reduce the document to 50 per cent so that it is easier to see. Save this under a name such as 'blank page template' because you will be using it again.

13 Using the two middle pages of the dummy book as your guide, match its page numbers with the page numbers in your main document and copy and paste the left-hand page into the left-hand column of the file and the right-hand page into the right-hand column. Use the return key to move the cursor to the top of the right-hand column if necessary.

14 Click on 'view' then 'headers and footers' and switch to footers. This will run across the bottom of the page. Put the left-hand number on the left-hand side page then move the cursor across to number the right-hand side page.

15 Save this file under its page numbers. If you have seven pages in your dummy book save it as 'pages 13 and 14'.

16 Delete this text from your template ready to use again. Turn your dummy page over and, using it as a guide, copy and paste the relevant pages from your main document as before then number them.

17 Repeat until all the pages have been copied and pasted into new files.

Printing

1 Print the first file you created, which will be the two centre pages.

2 Turn the page over and print the next file on the other side of the paper.

3 Repeat until all the files have been printed.

> **Top tip**
>
> Make sure you put the paper in the printer the right way up when you turn it over because it is easy to print the second side upside down.

Covers

To make a hard cover either use thin card – if your printer will allow this – or laminate a sheet of the same paper used for the book. If you don't have a laminator it is possible to have the covers laminated at a photocopying shop.

Cover design

If you have Microsoft Office Publisher you could choose one of the designs already set up in the software. When you have created the one you want, save it as a jpeg so that you can insert it as a picture on to your front page.

It is also easy to create your own design perhaps using a photo or drawing with the title etc. superimposed over it. Again, save it as a jpeg.

There is no need to waste the back page of the cover so this can be used for additional information or photographs – as can the two inside pages.

Printing

To create the cover the process is the same as for the pages. Open a new file, format the margins and insert two columns.

Insert your front cover photo into the right-hand column. Then insert the information or photo for the back page into the left-hand column.

Turn the page over and repeat the process if using the inside pages.

> **Top tip**
> Add extra interest to the cover by using either suitably coloured card or one with a faint pattern on.

Stapling

Collate the pages, fold in half and staple through the middle. This is called saddle-stitching – an unusual term, but there are special staplers called booklet staplers where the book is laid over a 'saddle' to be stapled. They can staple up to 25 sheets of paper – which is equivalent to a 100-page book, but don't forget to take into account the hard cover. At the time of writing it is possible to buy one for about £50.

The other ways of stapling are to use a long arm or long reach stapler, which are much less expensive, but again this may limit you to 25 sheets, or a high capacity staple gun which can staple up to 60 sheets.

Creep allowance

If you try to staple more than a few sheets together the inside pages will protrude or creep forward – this is called the creep allowance. Professionally stapled books counteract this by trimming off the excess paper to give a level edge. If there are only a few pages this can be done on a home paper trimmer or with a stout pair of scissors and a steady hand. Another alternative is a Stanley knife – use a metal ruler or something similar as a guide.

If you have a lot of books to trim it might be better to buy a proper guillotine. At the time of writing one which would trim 15 sheets, equivalent to 30 pages, costs around £50. Trimming means that the width of the outer margins of the pages nearer the centre will be slightly narrower.

A4 stapled booklet

This is created in the same way as above but you will need to photocopy the printed pages on a photocopier which can enlarge A4 sheets up to A3 size, so that when you fold them in half each page is A4 size.

> **Top tip**
>
> Because the pages will now be enlarged use a smaller font size such as 8 or 9.

A4 or A5 comb bound book

With this method the pages are bound together with a plastic-toothed roll. It is usually used for binding office reports or similar documents. Although your book will look less like a traditional book this method does have some advantages:

- It allows more pages – up to 145 sheets, which is 290 pages.
- It is simpler to format and print.
- Photos can be printed on glossy paper and kept separate from the text if wanted.
- It won't rust.
- There is no problem with creep allowance.
- It is fairly strong.

Formatting and printing

Put all the chapters into one document with page breaks between chapters. Allow sufficient margins to accommodate the plastic roll and justify the right-hand side. Print on both sides of each sheet. This can be done by stipulating in the 'page range' box on the Print menu all the odd number pages and then turning the pages round and printing all the even number pages. Or select the facility to print on both sides.

> **Top tip**
>
> If you have a lot of pages to print select 'print' from the menu, click on 'options' then tick 'reverse printing' box so that the pages will be printed starting with the last one, and end up in the right order.

This method can be used for printing life stories written to the formula in Chapter 03.

For an A5 comb bound book use the same method as above, but click on 'page set-up', then 'paper' and change the paper size to A5. You can then print on A5 paper.

Binding

At the time of writing it is possible to buy a comb binding machine for as little as £50. The other alternative is to have your books comb bound at a photocopying shop or office stationary suppliers.

A4 or A5 thermal bound book

Thermal binding uses heat to glue the pages together. This method creates a traditional looking book, but unless you can cover the glued edge it is a little unsightly and may not be as long lasting as saddle-stitching or comb binding. Thermal binding machines cost around £50 to buy but can bind up to 200 sheets of paper. To bind more you will need a more expensive machine.

Formatting and printing

Follow the method given for comb binding to create the pages.

A4 or A5 in ring binder

This is probably the easiest and cheapest method of all as ring binders are fairly inexpensive – but the finished result will look the least like a traditional book.

If possible choose ring binders with plastic pockets on the front and spine so that you can insert your own cover.

Formatting and printing

Follow the same methods for A4 or A5 comb bound pages.

Professional binding

This is the most expensive option, but you will end up with a book to be proud to have on your shelf – and if you only want a few copies for family and friends then this could be the option to go for. Look in the *Yellow Pages* to find a local bookbinder.

Summary

In this chapter you have learnt:

- how to create a book on a computer
- how to format
- various ways of binding.

20

blogging and other forms of publishing

In this chapter you will learn:
- different ways of recording your life story
- how to set up a blogging site
- how to popularize your site.

Everybody has a story to tell – 'everyone is a special kind of artist', even if they're not aware of it. For those to whom even writing a 'thank you' letter is a chore, the idea of writing an account of their own life in 60,000 words is an impossibility. But a chat with a friendly interviewer, recorded on tape or disc and then carefully transcribed, is a much easier way to achieve a good result. The spoken word is a very different medium to the written, but sometimes it can be more successful in conveying the unique voice of the subject. I recorded Miles Kington talking about his life in the weeks before he died in 2008, and those tapes are now a precious memorial for his family and friends.

Tony Staveacre

Up to this point the assumption has been that life stories are written out in book form, but of course there are other ways of recording them. These include:

- on a CD ROM
- on your website
- as a blog.

On a CD ROM

If your life story is already written out, or if you are an accomplished off-the-cuff speaker then you can record your story yourself.

Otherwise you will need someone to act as an interviewer asking you questions. This can be a friend or family member. Agree between you what the questions will be – or use some or all of the questions in Chapter 03.

You will need a proper mini-disc recorder, not a tape recorder or voice recorder, which at the time of writing could be bought for around £120.

It is possible to do basic editing, by marking edit points as you record. However, a better way is to download the recording from the mini-disc to your computer and then use an editing programme like Cool Edit to make any changes.

Once it is on your computer, provided you have a CD re-writer, you will also be able to burn more CDs to give or sell to family and friends. Making copies of CDs will work out cheaper than publishing a book and they are cheaper to post as well.

On your website

If you have your own website then why not upload your life story on to it. You may also be able to add photos and videos to illustrate it.

If you don't have a website it might be cheaper to set one up rather than pay to publish a book. Your Internet service provider (ISP) may offer space for free.

Uploading

Your story can be in one continuous piece, but surveys indicate that viewers don't like scrolling down, they prefer pages, so set up the website so that viewers can click to reach the next page.

As a blog

By far the easiest and cheapest way to publish your life story is to turn it into a blog. Although many people use blogging as a way of writing their daily diary, there is nothing to stop you uploading your life story to share with family, friends – and the world if you choose.

The word 'blog' is an abbreviation of weblog, and blogging is generally considered to be a way of writing thoughts and opinions on the Internet for others to read.

Using a personal website has been a popular way of keeping in touch for many years. Families who are spread around the world, travellers who wanted those back home to be able to keep up with their adventures, have used this method – which is quicker, easier, cheaper and probably more reliable than the post. Politicians, journalists, news presenters, business managers and celebrities also use them to get across their point of view.

But the phenomenon really took off with the advent of specialist blogging sites which made it easy for anyone and everyone to start writing. And of course, everyone did – and not only the young. People of all ages and from all walks of life have found blogging exciting and informative.

For some blogging is therapeutic – a way of sharing an often unimaginable burden of illness, loss or bereavement. For others it is a way of making friends and getting to know people from around the world, like Sally Crocker.

Case study

Sally's Chateau, the name of my blog, is part of the worldwide blogging phenomenon and originated, like so many blogs, completely by chance.

I am lucky and live in the most beautiful nineteenth-century house known as 'Le Chateau' near Carcassonne in the south-west of France. With stunning scenery, the sunflowers, vineyards and mountains, I draw my inspiration from my home and surroundings. With each blog posting I include a photograph, sometimes of the area, known as the Languedoc, the house or merely something I find interesting. I find posting a photograph to accompany my postings very popular amongst my readership, often just prompting the comment 'beautiful photograph'.

Since starting my blog I have become acquainted with people from all over the world. People that read the blog have also come and stayed at the house, but also what it has done is open up a whole new world for me. Through my blog I have pursued my love of writing and photography but most importantly it has boosted my self-confidence as I see my blogspot blossom and gain a following through my everyday tales of living in France. It has now become an enjoyable ritual. The benefit and beauty of blogging of course is that it is open to anyone, to pursue as often or little as they wish.

For anybody contemplating writing for personal enjoyment my advice would be, go for it, become a blogger!

Sally Crocker

Getting started

There are plenty of blogging sites to choose from many of which are free to use. It is worthwhile looking at a few sites to see which appeals and which you find easiest to use (see Appendices).

If you don't want to share your life story with everyone choose a site which has privacy settings. This allows you to control who has access to your blog. Let your family and friends know where to find it and give them the password.

> **Top tip**
>
> Never put anything on a blog that you wouldn't put in a book. You might get sued.

As one of the main advantages blogging has over conventional publishing is the facility to upload videos as well as photos, make sure the site you choose allows you to do this.

Having chosen your host site you will need to choose a 'log in' name. Once logged on you will be offered a choice of ready-made templates, which can be personalized.

> **Top tip**
>
> Never reveal personal details on a blogging site which is open to all and sundry as this could lead to identity fraud.

Uploading

When you check the blogging sites you will see that most blogs are comparatively short. If you are restricting your site to family and friends they will be interested in reading longer entries, but if you intend your site to be read by the public it is better to keep each entry short, say one chapter at a time.

In this way your book will read more like a serial. And you will be in good company if you do this; many of Charles Dickens' novels were first published in magazines in serial form.

Getting known

If you want your site read by as many people as possible you will need to actively promote it. It can take up to a year to get noticed and start to build up a following.

There are several ways of getting your blog known:

- Email as many people as you can telling them where to find your blog and ask them to pass the information on to their friends.
- Register your blog with specialist search engines (see Appendix B).
- Make sure you get picked up by search engines by having key words in your titles which relate to the content of your blog.
- Choose a catchy title for your blog.
- Write regularly: if you have attracted an audience then they will want to keep coming back for more.
- Join online forums related to your blog.
- Post on other blogs and ask friendly bloggers to include you in their blogroll (a list of their favourite sites) and do the same for them.
- Upload photos and videos.

So if your aim is to make your life story available without going to the expense of paying for publication then blogging could be the answer.

Summary

In this chapter you have learnt:

- how to record your life story on CD ROM
- about blogging
- how to use your blogging site.

section five

more strings to your bow

21

further writing opportunities

In this chapter you will learn:
- how to write biographies
- how to collect information
- how to interview your subject.

It is absurd to divide people into good and bad. People are either charming or tedious.

Oscar Wilde

Now that you have a book under your belt it could open up other doors for you. The skills you have picked up writing your life story can be used to help other people write theirs. Or you could become a ghost writer and write their life story for them.

You might also want to consider writing biographies which is just someone else's life story told in the third person.

Writing biographies

Although you might start with family and friends there is nothing to stop you writing about anyone that interests you, provided you can obtain all the information and documents needed to describe their life.

Be aware though that with some subjects you may also need their permission, or the permission of their heirs, to write it. Not everyone wants a biography written about them, or a member of their family, and some go to great lengths to prevent it. Other people want to choose their biographer and will only grant that person access to family documents and no one else. Their wishes do get ignored and you do find books described as 'the unofficial biography of X', but if you decide to go down this route be prepared to face difficulties and possibly hostility.

Your choice of who to write about may also be dictated by whether or not you want to have the biography published. If you have found an interesting relative or ancestor while researching your life story and just wish to write their story for the family that's fine.

But if you want to get a conventional publisher interested, your subject will need to be someone that the public will want to read about. This doesn't necessarily mean they have to be a household name, but they do need to have done something with their lives which makes them fascinating.

Top tip

Choose someone you are interested in, whether or not you like them, otherwise you won't enjoy the work involved.

And finding a publisher comes before you write the biography, because if no one is interested in taking it up there is no point in writing it – unless you are going to self publish instead. However, you will still have to do sufficient research to enable yourself to put together an attractive proposal.

Research publishers in the same way as for publishing a life story, see Chapter 16.

Collecting information

Your first task is to collect as much information as possible by:

- interviews
- accessing documents
- research.

Interviews

If the subject is a family member or friend this will probably be easy to arrange. If you are writing about a stranger then you will need to contact them, or their heirs if applicable, and make an appointment.

Face-to-face interviews are the best, but if the distance involved makes this impossible then do them by letter, email or phone.

When doing an interview bear the following in mind:

- Let the subject choose how and where to be interviewed.
- Be punctual, whether it is a face-to-face interview or by phone: if it is by phone it should be on your phone bill.
- Have more than one pen with you.
- If you have a recorder ask if you can record the interview to either save taking notes or as a back-up.
- Have a list of questions ready to ask so that you don't waste time, but be prepared to follow another line of questioning if the subject reveals information you didn't know about.
- Don't talk about yourself, unless you are trying to put the subject at their ease.
- Don't let the interview go on too long. If you said it would only last an hour then end it after an hour unless the subject is genuinely happy to continue.
- Remember to ask if you can contact them for further interviews and to clarify any points made.

Probing questions

Although you will have your prepared questions such as all the important dates, relationships, turning points etc., you will also need to decide whether to ask the more probing questions. The answers to these could be the ones which reveal your subject's motivations and deep-seated fears and anxieties, but they may also cause the subject to terminate the interview.

You will need to establish trust between you and your subject, so that they have confidence in the way you are going to write about them. Start by asking non-controversial questions and gauge the subject's answers and body language to see how far your questioning can go. There is no point in alienating them to the extent that they will no longer co-operate with you.

Accessing documents

These will be the same kind of documents which you researched for your life story: diaries, letters etc., see Chapter 02. If your subject is dead you may have to ask their family for access to documents and other archival material. Some material may also be held in public record offices.

Research

Again this will be the same as you carried out for your life story, see Chapters 04 and 05. It will also include reading other biographies, both about your subject and those which mention them.

If your subject was born more than 100 years ago, you will need to research the society into which they were born and the culture and habits of that time as well as local, national and worldwide events which had a bearing on their lives.

Writing

Your biography can be about the full life of your subject or a section of it. It can be written in chronological order, around themes and topics, in flashbacks or by vignettes. Follow the same processes as you did for writing your life story, see Chapters 08, 09 and 10. You will also need to give it readability, see Chapter 11. Read as many different biographies as you can to pick up ideas on the best way of presenting your subject.

However, as well as knowing all the relevant details about where they were born etc. the reader will also want to know what makes your subject tick. What forces shaped their lives and made them the type of person they became. If they are still alive you will be able to ask them. If they are dead then perhaps their family will be able to answer those questions. Otherwise you will need to make your own judgement.

The other main difference between writing a life story and a biography is that the biography will be filtered through you and your opinions and experiences. Also, as the biographer, you will not only be presenting a person's life, but will also be analyzing their motives, assessing their achievements and trying to explain why they acted as they did.

Their life also need to be explained in the context of the times, society and culture in which they were living. Guard against making judgements which would be applicable today, but not when they were alive. Sometimes it is only hindsight which enables the biographer to make sense of their subject's life.

> **Top tip**
> Whether or not you like your subject, be objective and honest in your writing.

Summary

In this chapter you have learnt:

- about establishing trust
- when to ask probing questions
- what to include.

22

giving talks

In this chapter you will learn:
- how to get started
- how to prepare your talk
- techniques for speaking.

It usually takes me more than three weeks to prepare a good impromptu speech.

Mark Twain

As well as the skills to write more books you now have the basis for giving several talks including:

- your own life story
- how to write a life story
- how to research family history
- how to publish a book.

Getting started

Most groups which have regular speakers at their meetings are desperate for new faces, and once you become known you will probably be inundated with requests. However, everyone has to get a foot on the ladder, so approach groups that you know and offer to give them a talk. Then if they are asked by another group for details of willing speakers they will pass your name across. You can also advertise in the local press. Bear in mind that many groups book speakers up to a year in advance – although there are occasionally last-minute cancellations when you may be able to step into the breach.

Preparing your talk

Decide which of your subjects you are going to talk about and pick the most interesting or dramatic aspects of it. Put these into a logical order then divide them into short sections. Write a sentence for each section on three inch × five inch cards to act as crib cards or memory aids.

Top tip

Number the cards so that if you drop them you can easily put them back in the right order.

Structuring your talk

The talks suggested at the beginning of this chapter are either going to be informative or entertaining or both. So you want to keep the tone light. Alert the audience to this by starting the talk with an amusing anecdote or story, or some interesting statistics. The audience can then relax and start to enjoy themselves.

The rest of your talk should follow on in chronological order. Depending on the subject it could consist almost entirely of anecdotes.

Top tip

Most talks benefit from some anecdotes or stories.

Try to round off your talk with a good ending rather than petering out as if you have run out of steam. You could briefly sum up what your talk was about, or explain any lessons learned, or end with another anecdote.

Practice makes perfect

Practise your talk until you don't need to rely on your cards. Record your talk so that you can hear what it will sound like. Stand in front of a mirror to check that you are not waving your hands about or doing anything else which could distract your audience. When you feel confident, give your talk to a friend or member of your family and ask for objective feedback.

Illustrating your talk

Most talks benefit from being illustrated. If you are using slides make sure you have them the right way up and the right way round. Again it is a good idea to number them as well as naming them just in case they get spilled. Photographs can also be displayed using PowerPoint via a computer – check that the venue has the necessary facilities.

Top tip

Thorough preparation gives confidence.

Practicalities

When you have been asked to give a talk you need to check the following:

- Your contact: Do you have their name and phone number in case you are held up and running late?
- The venue: If you are not sure exactly where it is ask the organizer to send directions. If you have the postcode you will be able to find it with sat nav or using one of the Internet sites which give you maps and instructions.
- Car parking: Not all venues have car parks and it may take extra time to find somewhere to park. Also you may be carrying equipment if the venue doesn't provide it so check whether you can temporarily park outside to unload.
- The date, including the year: Checking the year may sound odd, but some organizations book their speakers more than a year in advance. I once turned up at a village hall to talk to the local Women's Institute group only to find it closed up and empty. When I contacted the chairman to find out where everyone was she confirmed that I had the day and the month right, but I was a year early! She hadn't realized she hadn't specified which year and it hadn't occurred to me to ask.
- The time: Depending on the type of organization, they may go through an agenda first. Find out what time you will be expected to speak as well as what time the meeting starts.
- How long they want you to speak for: Most talks last about 45 minutes.
- Will they want you to answer questions from the floor.
- The size of the room: If it is large you may need a microphone. Ask if the venue has sound facilities or whether you need to organize a microphone. If they are providing the mike will it be on a stand, hand-held, clipped to your tie or top, or a face mike?
- How many people will be attending: If you are planning to hand out any information or business cards you will need to take enough for everyone.
- If you have a book to sell, check that the group is happy for you to bring copies along to sell at the meeting.
- What equipment the venue is able to provide: You can then decide what you will need to take with you. You may prefer to take your own slide projector rather than struggle to use an unfamiliar one.

What to wear

Wear clothes that make you feel confident. These should be comfortable, but smart. For women, unless you find it hard to do without high heels it might be safer to wear something with a lower heel – you may have to climb up on to a stage.

Giving the talk

Most people are nervous the first time they have to stand up in front of a room full of people and to talk to them for 45 minutes. But don't forget the audience won't know this is your first talk – unless you tell them – so speak confidently. Remember the audience is on your side and wants you to succeed. In fact, if they do know this is your first time they may be more nervous than you, so put them at their ease.

Have your memory aid cards close at hand even if you don't expect to use them. Then if you dry up you can have a quick glance at them. If you do use them try to get into the habit of glancing at them quickly and then looking straight back at the audience before speaking. Don't look down at the card and speak while you are reading it – the audience will only hear a mumble.

Don't talk to just one person or one section of the room but make sure you look at all parts of the room while you are speaking. Try to make eye contact to keep everyone's attention.

> **Top tip**
> Don't pick a spot on the wall at the back of the room and talk over people's heads – your audience will start to lose interest.

If you don't have a microphone aim your voice at the person sitting furthest away: it is not always the volume which makes it easy for people to hear, but pitch and clarity.

Speak naturally and speak slowly, but not to the extent that it sounds as if you are teaching a lesson to five-year-olds.

If the venue allows, you might find it helpful to move around rather than standing still.

Getting started

It is normal to be a little bit nervous – any actor or competitor will tell you that you need a bit of adrenalin to perform to the best of your ability. When it is your turn to speak, take one or two deep breaths, thank the person who introduced you and then wait a few seconds while your audience settles – you could even take a sip of water while you wait if your mouth has gone dry.

> **Top tip**
> It is better not to have any alcohol beforehand, but if you do need some Dutch courage, make it a small one.

If you are good at telling jokes then that can be a good way to get the audience warmed up and receptive. But telling jokes well is quite a skill so if you know you're not good at it then don't. A joke told badly will get you off to a poor start. The wrong joke to the wrong audience will get you off to a very poor start.

Depending on how much information your host has given the audience in their introduction, you may have to give some explanation about your talk or some background detail before you start the talk proper.

> **Top tip**
> If it is a warm room and an elderly audience don't be surprised if one or two nod off – it does happen.

Answering questions

Most talks are followed by questions from the audience, but if you find that people are reluctant to ask any, don't look around the room desperately – have some questions ready on your memory cards and pose one or two yourself. For example you could say, 'I am often asked how easy it is to write a life story and I say…' This will then trigger questions from the audience.

Extras

Charging a fee

Some speakers make a charge for their talks, and most groups will offer to pay. Whether you decide to charge, and how much, is down to you, but don't price yourself out of the market. Many speakers give talks in aid of their pet charity. Or you can ask the organization to donate your fee to a charity of their choice.

Expenses

Most groups offer expenses – don't feel bad about taking them now that it costs so much to travel anywhere.

Giving talks can be great fun. You will undoubtedly meet lots of interesting people and your experiences could even form the basis of another book.

Summary

In this chapter you have learnt:

- how to use crib cards
- how to illustrate your talk
- how to handle questions.

Standard guidelines for magazine articles

Use good quality A4 white paper then:

- Set up wide margins all round on all pages.
- Double space the text.
- Leave two double spaces between paragraphs.
- Indent the first line of each paragraph.
- Number the pages and show how many pages there are altogether, for example, *page 1 of 8.*
- Don't let paragraphs run across from one page to the next.
- Put the title on each page, preferably at the top.
- Put *more* or *mf* (meaning 'more follows'), at bottom right of each page except the last.
- Put *ends* on the last page at the end of the article.
- After *ends* put your contact details, word count and whether you are including photographs.

Below are three sample guidelines, however it is always worth checking with your chosen magazine for their specific requirements.

Non-fiction guidelines for *Yours* magazine (courtesy of *Yours* magazine)

Every article is read with interest but the Features department receives more than 100 manuscripts a month, and is able to publish only one a fortnight. The queue is long, so please allow up to three months for a reply.

- Submissions should be up to 950 words approx for a one-page article, and up to 1,300 for two pages. It is rare for *Yours* to read, or to publish any article of greater length than this.

- Manuscripts must be typed on one side of the paper and the title page should include: an accurate word count and your full name, address and telephone number.

- **Please try to enclose relevant photographs to illustrate your article, marked with your name and address on the back.**

- You should include a short CV of yourself, together with a clear, colour, head and shoulder picture of yourself. Again, please mark on the reverse with your name, address and telephone number.

- Your article will either be returned to you as unsuitable (providing you remember an sae!) or we will let you know that it has been put on hold for a few months, for possible future use. NB: This will give no guarantee of publication.

IMPORTANT

- Any article submitted must not have been published elsewhere and, if published by us, becomes exclusive to *Yours* magazine on an all-rights basis.

- *Yours* magazine reserves the right to edit, alter or shorten any article submitted and it may not appear in its entirety and it may appear in any of our publications.

- Although all reasonable care is taken, *Yours* magazine can assume no responsibility for the safety of unsolicited articles or photographs, so it is a good idea to send copies. Please enclose a stamped addressed envelope if you would like your manuscript returned.

KNOW YOUR AUDIENCE

Before submitting any articles, it is essential that you study at least six issues of *Yours* magazine. Most submissions are rejected because the subject matter and/or the style of writing, is unsuitable for readers.

Reading back issues will give you a good idea of the sort of person who reads *Yours* and the general tone we use – which is informal and chatty.

SUBJECTS

We are currently looking for reader stories on nostalgia only – we would particularly like to hear about your 1950s and 1960s experiences – and childhood.

STYLE AND TONE

Your article should grab the reader from the first sentence. Our style is friendly and warm – after all, your contributions are what makes *Yours* the magazine it is! And 400,000 readers a fortnight can't be wrong.

Send your manuscript to:

Yours Magazine
Bauer London Lifestyle,
Media House,
Peterborough Business Park,
Peterborough, PE2 6EA

Marking the envelope: Non Fiction Submission

Or by email to: **yours@bauerconsumer.co.uk** (Subject: Non Fiction Submission)

*PLEASE NOTE: If you would like us to return your submission, please include an sae with the correct postage amount on it. We regret that any submissions without an sae will not be returned.

Non-fiction guidelines for *The Oldie* magazine (courtesy of *The Oldie* magazine)

We are happy to consider unsolicited articles on any subject. Articles should be between 600 and 1,300 words in length, typed and accompanied by an sae.

Please send to:

Jeremy Lewis, Features Editor,
The Oldie,
65 Newman Street,
London, W1T 3EG.

You can also submit pieces by email. Please send to **jeremylewis@theoldie.co.uk**. Please attach pieces as Word documents, making sure that the document itself contains all your contact details.

Well-written articles on any subject are always welcome, and we are particularly interested in pieces for our 'I Once Met', and 'rant' slots. If photographs or illustrations accompany your piece, please send copies and not originals. We will contact you if we need to use originals for reproduction purposes. *The Oldie* cannot be held responsible for the loss or damage of any unsolicited materials.

Submitting articles – What we DON'T want:

We DO NOT accept poetry or short stories. We also do not commission pieces from treatments, only from assessing finished articles. It's also probably not worth telephoning the office to 'run an idea past us', the tale is almost always in the telling, and we'll always say the same thing: 'We can't promise anything, but if you're familiar with the magazine then please do have a go and send it to us, and we'll happily read it.' Also, please don't call and say 'I know you don't accept poetry, but I'd just like to read you this funny poem I've written anyway.' That would be greatly appreciated.

POLITE NOTICE: Please do not submit anything to us unless you have read at least two or three copies of *The Oldie* and have a good feel for the magazine. *The Oldie* is one of the very few magazines in the country who believe in dedicating time and effort from our limited resources to reading all unsolicited pieces, so please do your bit, pay attention to these guidelines and make sure you're familiar with the magazine. We only read unsolicited pieces one day a week, so replies can take a month or so.

Non-fiction guidelines for *The Scots Magazine* (courtesy of *The Scots Magazine*)

EDITORIAL GUIDELINES

The Scots Magazine has a team of regular professional contributors, but is also keen to encourage the submission of material from all writers and photographers. The following notes provide some basic guidelines.

GENERAL

We are a publication concerned with specifically Scottish topics... There is a minimum of four months between acceptance and publication: please take this into account if an article is aimed at a particular issue. It is not unusual for material to remain in stock for up to two years before publication.

Manuscripts should be typed, double spaced, with a substantial margin, and only on one side of the paper. The first page should start halfway down to allow for typesetting instructions.

Any relevant photographs, drawings, maps, diagrams, etc., should be enclosed with the text, and each item must bear the contributor's name and that of the copyright holder if different. Each illustration should also carry a brief caption explaining its significance in the article. Writers receive proofs to check, prior to the publication of articles. We prefer articles with a word count of around 1,000–2,500 words, but these limits are not rigid. We do not buy material that has already been published elsewhere. An sae with submissions is appreciated.

It should be borne in mind that this page is not a plea for material, rather a collection of hints on how to improve the chances of success. *The Scots Magazine's* acceptance rate of speculative submissions is less than five per cent – but you could be in that number.

GETTING THE FLAVOUR

Before writing for any publication it is essential to know the type of material it uses. By reading *The Scots Magazine* every month you will absorb our style and become familiar with the type of topics we deal with. As a bonus, you won't need to buy one if you're successful, for we send a complimentary copy of the issue with your article in it. Use the subscriptions coupon in the magazine to have a copy sent to you for 12 months.

PAYMENT

Articles are paid on acceptance. Illustrations, however, are paid on publication as the number we can use is not known until the page make-up has been completed.

COPYRIGHT

The Scots Magazine buys first copyright only, so that once we have printed your material you are free to offer it for publication elsewhere. When submitting photographs and other illustrations whose copyright is not held by the sender, it is incumbent on the contributor to obtain permission for their possible use in *The Scots Magazine*.

PHOTOGRAPHS

We can cope with all sizes and formats, but for colour we prefer original transparencies of 35 mm and upwards. All material is returned to photographers after publication. Please enclose a suitable sae for this purpose. Digital images must be high resolution pictures. (Our 'Photography Guidelines' contain more information.)

EDITING

Don't worry about spelling or grammar if you think you have an article worth writing, for all material is thoroughly sub-edited before publication. In the course of preparation, even professional texts have to be reduced or altered and you should not expect your author's proofs to be word for word with your manuscript. You may also be asked to elaborate on certain passages or add new paragraphs.

PRELIMINARY APPROACH

If you wish guidance on any aspect of contributing, *The Scots Magazine* staff will be pleased to help you. Write to us at:

The Scots Magazine,
D.C. Thomson & Co Ltd,
2 Albert Square,
Dundee, DD1 9QJ.
Email: **mail@scotsmagazine.com**

appendix b: useful websites

These are listed in chapter order.

Chapter 01 defining your reasons

www.amazon.co.uk Site for new and second-hand books.

www.amazon.com American site for new and second-hand books.

http://gifts.barnesandnoble.com American site for new and second-hand books.

Chapter 02 making a start

www.rogerco.freeserve.co.uk/index.htm (then click on 'date an old photo') A useful site which illustrates the typical clothes and hairstyles of the people ranging from 1860 to 1952. It also gives advice on dating professional photos by their shape.

www.fashion-era.com/ Contains a wealth of information about fashion and social history from 1800 onwards.

www.cyber-heritage.co.uk/women Magazine adverts from some of the women's magazines of the 1920s, 1930s and 1940s.

www.1940.co.uk Information about the 1940s.

www.whirligig-tv.co.uk Information about radio and television in the 1950s.

www.bbc.co.uk/cult/ilove/years Reference site for information about the 1960s, 1970s, 1980s and 1990s.

www.onlineweb.com/theones Lists the number one record in the pop charts from 1950 to 2000.

www.1920-30.com Site covering all aspects of the 'roaring twenties'.

www.bestofbritishmag.co.uk Magazine which includes readers' memories.

Chapter 03 writing to a formula

www.therememberingsite.org/ An American site where subscribers can answer a list of questions to help them write their life story.

Chapter 04 background research

Tracing people

www.friendsreunited.co.uk Site for reuniting people.

www.oldschoolmates.co.uk Site for tracing school friends.

http://people.yahoo.com/ American site for tracing addresses.

www.theukelectoralroll.co.uk/ This site also has data on The National Burial Index and the ownership of all UK property.

http://gov-reports.net American site for searching millions of government documents.

Old newspapers

www.iln.org.uk Site for old London Illustrated News papers from 1842 which gives the major events for each year.

www.newspaperarchive.com/Default.aspx American website for accessing old newspapers. There is a charge.

www.world-newspapers.com/about.html Lists dozens of newspapers and magazines from around the world and allows access to some of the articles.

www.greatexperiencedays.co.uk/pages/newspapers.asp Site which sells old copies of the *Times* dating from 1900.

www.newsrecreated.co.uk/ Site which sells books based on newspaper articles going back 100 years. The books are based on topics such as sport or historical stories.

www.bl.uk British Library site which includes newspaper archives.

www.reminisce.com American site for old magazine information.

Armed forces information

www.soldiermagazine.co.uk/flashback/idx.htm Contains 350 articles written between 1945 and 2005.

www.janes-defence-weekly.com/ Information about the weekly magazine.

www.rafa.org.uk/index.asp Amongst other information the site gives details of how to get in touch with local RAFA groups.

www.britisharmedforces.org This site contains a wealth of information, including stories from members of the armed forces.

www.firstworldwar.com This site contains amongst other information, personal letters and diaries from combatants and dozens of old photographs.

http://timewitnesses.org/english/ Stories from World War II.

www.firstworldwar.com Information from World War I.

www.bbc.co.uk/ww2peopleswar/ Contains a wealth of information based on personal recollections from 47,000 people.

www.1940.co.uk/ Information about World War II.

www.wartimememories.co.uk This site has dozens of wartime stories and is asking for more memories. Photos of former comrades can be uploaded for identification as well as requests for information on them.

http://timewitnesses.org/english Site which has war stories from other countries as well as the UK.

www.gulfveteransassociation.co.uk/index.htm Information about the Gulf War veterans.

Local history

www.local-history.co.uk/Groups/ Gives contact details of some local history groups.

Photos, postcards and theatre memorabilia

www.footstepsphotos.co.uk Photos available dating from 1900 to 1930.

www.photo-ark.co.uk/html Old photos. Site also has artists' sketches and old maps.

www.oldukphotos.com/ A resource site for old photos – they are not for sale.

www.istockphoto.com Resource site for old photos.

www.collectbritain.co.uk/collections/ Part of the British Library, this site has various collections including old maps and photos.

www.postcardworld.co.uk Old postcards available to buy.

www.oldpostcardsforsale.com/index.htm Old postcards available to buy.

www.oldcards.co.uk Useful site as postcards are dived into counties.

www.shilohpostcards.net American site for postcards.

www.thepostcard.com American site for postcards.

www.bristol.ac.uk/theatrecollection/ Site has information about the British theatre.

www.nls.uk/collections/british/scottish_theatres_database.html Site has information about the theatre in Scotland.

www.c20th.com Site for theatre memorabilia.

www.eBay.co.uk/ Even if you don't want to buy anything there are lots of interesting items for sale which could trigger memories.

Back-up and data saving services

www.backupdirect.net Stores data for you.

www.datafort.co.uk Stores data for you.

www.securstore.com Stores data for you.

www.thinkingsafe.com Stores data for you.

www.adept-telecom.co.uk Stores data for you.

http://www.databarracks.com Stores data for you.

www.pro-net.co.uk Stores data for you.

www.storegate.co.uk Stores data for you.

Chapter 05 researching the family tree

www.genuki.org.uk Describes itself as a 'virtual reference library' and the site contains many useful links as well as information on researching family trees.

www.nationalarchives.gov.uk/ This site has a wealth of information on all aspects for researching the family tree.

www.familysearch.org This is the website for The Church of Jesus Christ of Latter-day Saints.

www.thegenealogist.co.uk Has many searchable databases. Pay-as-you-go or a monthly subscription, at time of writing from £4.66.

www.findmypast.com Has many searchable databases including living people finder. Pay-to-view or by subscription.

www.rootsuk.com/ Search by using credits, minimum payment £5.

www.genesreunited.co.uk/ As well as accessing data, this site allows you to get in touch with other researchers.

www.ancestry.co.uk Includes censuses for England, Scotland and Wales as well as some military records.

www.ancestry.com/ This is the American site for the US census collection, birth, marriage and death certificates, military records and other databases, including One World Tree.

www.freerecordsregistry.com An American site for searching for birth, marriage and death certificates.

www.public-files.com An American site for searching for birth, marriage and death certificates.

www.jewishgen.org A resource site for Jewish genealogy, also has a list of databases.

www.britishdataarchive.com Sells CD ROMs of censuses by year and county. Not all are available yet.

www.originsnetwork.com This site has many different databases online such as wills as well as old photographs and books. Subscriptions are for unlimited access for three days or one month.

www.theukelectoralroll.co.uk/ This site offers electoral roll and electoral register searches by forename, surname, address, births, deaths, marriages and property ownership to instantly find anyone in the UK. The site also includes the National Burial Index.

www.rootsweb.ancestry.com/ Resource site for researching family trees.

www.cyndislist.com/ A resource site which cross-references other genealogical sites from around the world.

www.olivetreegenealogy.com A resource site which cross-references other genealogical sites in Canada and America.

http://usgenweb.org/ An American website which contains a wealth of information on tracing family trees in each state.

www.mdgenweb.org The site for tracing family trees in the American state of Maryland.

www.findagrave.com American website containing millions of cemetery records.

http://projectbritain.com/ Click on 'Royalty' for a timeline of English kings and queens.

www.oz.net/~markhow/englishros.htm Names and addresses of most of the county public record offices.

Chapter 06 how to write an article from your life story

www.bartleby.com/ A site which allows you to read extracts from Ulysses S. Grant's war memoirs which some consider to be the best ever written.

Magazines which take articles

www.parkpublications.co.uk Publishes UK magazine *Country Tales*, four times a year in A5 format and paid for by subscription. Takes articles up to 1,500 words, that have a rural theme.

www.chapman-pub.co.uk *Chapman*, a Scottish magazine printed three times a year. Interested in new writers.

www.mslexia.co.uk *Mslexia*, a magazine for women published quarterly.

www.family-tree.co.uk *Family Tree,* published monthly, takes articles, but has a backlog.

www.theoldie.co.uk *The Oldie,* published monthly.

www.bestofbritishmag.co.uk/ *Best of British*, a monthly magazine which welcomes articles and letters from readers about their memories. There is also a section where readers can ask for help in tracing long lost friends and family as well as information.

www.yours.co.uk/Yours-Magazine/ *Yours*, a fortnightly magazine for women over the age of 50 and its sister website. Memories can be downloaded on to the website and the magazine welcomes articles and letters.

www.uniquemagazines.co.uk publishes several magazines, including *The People's Friend*, *Down Your Way* and *Dalesman*.

www.reminisce.com/ *Reminisce*, an American magazine which accepts true-life stories.

www.retiredmagazines.co.uk/forums/ Internet site where visitors can upload their memories or true life stories.

www.scotsmagazine.com/ Welcomes articles with a Scottish flavour.

Writing groups

www.nawg.co.uk Site for the National Association of Writers Groups. Gives information on existing groups.

http://youwriteon.com/ Site sponsored by Arts Council, which amongst other information has some details of writers' groups.

www.bbc.co.uk/learning/coursesearch/get_writing/ Has information on creative writing courses by area.

http://writers.meetup.com/ American site for finding writers' groups.

Chapter 13 grammar

www.uefap.com/writing Useful information on grammar.

www.ssdd.uce.ac.uk/learner Useful information on grammar.

www.buzzin.net/english Useful information on grammar.

www.studygs.net/wrtstr6.htm Useful information on transitional words.

www.phon.ucl.ac.uk Useful information on grammar.

http://dictionary.reference.com An American site which includes dictionary and thesaurus.

Chapter 18 self publishing

http://www.inprint.co.uk/thebookguide/index.shtml. Useful information site including a list of regional bookbinders.

Self publishing companies

http://youwriteon.com/ Site sponsored by Arts Council, which offers self publishing.

www.rossendalebooks.co.uk Offers self publishing.

www.modernmemoirs.com/philosophy.html Offers self publishing.

http://website.lineone.net/~selfpublishuk/index.htm The self publishing part of Emissary Publishing.

www.selfpublishing.co.uk Offers self publishing.

www.netcomuk.co.uk Offers self publishing.

www.ondemandbooks.co.uk Offers self publishing.

www.bookofmylife.co.uk Offers self publishing.

www.authorhouse.co.uk/GetPublished Offers self publishing.

www.modernmemoirs.com An American site offering self publishing facilities.

www.woodfieldpublishing.co.uk Interested in memoirs.

Chapter 21 further writing opportunities

Blogging sites

www.thoughts.com/free-blog Allows you to see what other bloggers are writing before you sign up.

www.blogger.com One of the best-known sites for free blogging now owned by Google™.

www.typepad.com Paid for site.

http://freeblogit.com Allows you to see what other bloggers are writing before you sign up.

www.saga.co.uk Click on 'community' to join the Saga Zone blogging site.

www.facebook.com Allows privacy control.

www.livejournal.com Allows privacy control.

www.blog.myspace.com/ One of the most popular with teenagers.

www.youtube.com/ Used more for downloading videos.

Books

Adolph, Anthony, *Tracing your Family History*, Collins, 2004

Atchity, Kenneth, *A Writer's Time*, W. W. Norton and Company, 1995

Chalker, Jack, *Burma Railway, Images of War*, Mercer Books, 2007

Chisholm, Alison and Coutrie, Brenda, *How to Write About Yourself*, Allison and Busby, 1999

Colwell, Stella, *Teach Yourself Tracing Your Family History*, Hodder Education, 2007

Daniel, Lois, *How to Write your own Life Story*, Chicago Review Press, fourth edition 1997

Ferris, Stewart, *How to get Published*, Summersdale Publishers Ltd, 2005

Frances, Mary, *Song of the Spinning Sun*, Trafford Publishing, 2007

Gilbert, Frances, *I'm a Teacher Get Me Out of Here*, Short Books, 2005

Hey, David, *Journeys in Family History*, The National Archives, 2004

Hoffman, Ann, *Research for Writers*, A & C Black, seventh edition 2003

Hunt, F. W. 'Mike', *Mike's Memoirs*, Woodfield Publishing, Bognor Regis, 2004

Kilvert, Francis, *Kilvert's Diary 1870–1879*, Penguin, 1977 (a selection edited by William Plomer)

Lucas, Mary, *Lunchmeat and Life Lessons,* MBL Books, 2006

Marelli, Diane, *Meet Your Ancestors*, How to Books Ltd, reprint 2004

Mostafa, Joshua, *Desktop Publishing,* Dorling Kindersley, 2000

Nobbs, David, *I didn't get where I am Today*, Arrow Books, 2003

Oke, Michael, *Write your Life Story*, How to Books Ltd, revised 2006

Titford, John, *Writing up Your Family History*, Countryside Books, 2005

Walker, Graham, *Unsettled*, Tangent Books, Bristol, 2007

Watts, Nigel, *Teach Yourself Writing a Novel*, Hodder Headline, 2003

Westcott, Arthur, *Arthur's Village,* published by Congresbury History Society, 2003

Books referred to as examples:

A Child called It by Dave Pelzer

Adolph Hitler: My Part in his Downfall; Mussolini: His Part in my Downfall by Spike Milligan

A Lotus Grows in the Mud by Goldie Hawn

American Hostage by Micah Garan and Marie-Hélène Carleton

And when did you last see your Father? by Blake Morrison

A Royal Duty by Paul Burrell

A Walk in the Woods by Bill Bryson

A Year in Provence by Peter Mayle

A Year in the Merde by Stephen Clarke

Behind Closed Doors by Jenny Tomlin

Bravo Two Zero by Andy McNab

Diana's Story by Deric Longden

Don't Tell Mummy by Toni Maguire

Enough about Me by Jancee Dunn

Eragon by Christopher Paolin

Extreme by Sharon Osbourne

French Leave by John Burton Race

Help Yourself by Dave Pelzer

High Adventure by Edmund Hilary

Mad, Bad and Dangerous to Know by Ranulph Fiennes

Marley and Me by John Grogan

Memoirs of Richard Nixon by Richard Nixon

My Side by David Beckham

My Spy: Memoir of a CIA Wife by Bina Cady Kiyonaga

My Turn to make the Tea by Monica Dickens

Neither Here nor There: Travels around Europe by Bill Bryson

Notes from a small Soprano by Lesley Garrett

One Pair of Hands, One Pair of Feet by Monica Dickens

Open Secret by Stella Rimmington

Ricky by Ricky Tomlinson

Ring of Bright Water by Gavin Maxwell

Shadowmancer by Graham Taylor

Some other Rainbow John McCarthy & Jill Morrell

The Life and Times of the Thunderbolt Kid by Bill Bryson

The Thrush Green and Fairacre series by Miss Read

The Virgin Soldiers by Leslie Thomas

Toast by Nigel Slater

Touching the Void by Joe Simpson

Tuesdays with Morrie by Mitch Albom

Vets Might Fly by James Herriot

Magazines

Writing Magazine
Warners Group Publications plc,
5th floor, 31–32 Park Row,
Leeds,
West Yorkshire, LS1 5JD
www.writingmagazine.co.uk

Monthly magazine available in newsagents.

Family Tree magazine
61 Great Whyte,
Ramsey,
Huntingdon,
Cambridgeshire, PE26 1HJ
www.family-tree.co.uk

Monthly magazine available in newsagents.

The Self Publishing Magazine
9 De Montfort Mews,
Leicester, LE1 7FW
www.troubador.co.uk/selfpublishingmagazine

Published by Troubador the magazine comes out three times a year and is available on subscription.

Yours magazine
Bauer,
Media House,
Peterborough Business Park,
Peterborough, PE2 6EA
www.yours.co.uk

Published fortnightly by Bauer the magazine is available in newsagents.

index